Bringing Back the Bones

NEW AND SELECTED POEMS

Gary Fincke

Stephen F. Austin State University Press
Nacogdoches, Texas

For more information:
Stephen F. Austin State University Press
P.O. Box 13007 SFA Station
Nacogdoches, Texas 75962
sfapress@sfasu.edu
www.sfasu.edu/sfapress

Book design: Asha Layeni-Gardner
Cover design: Asha Layeni-Gardner
Distrubted by Texas A&M Consortium
www.tamupress.com

LIBRARY OF CONGRESS CATALOGING-IN-PUBLICATION DATA
Fincke, Gary
Bringing Back the Bones / Gary Fincke
p.cm.

ISBN: 978-1-62288-111-6

Additional Praise for Bringing Back the Bones

"I am moved by how deeply these poems engage working class experiences. The poems honor the life lived . . . they are to be remembered."

Edward Hirsch, author of *Gabriel: A Poem*

"Romantic, preternaturally alert . . . and as drawn to wisdom as to comedy, Fincke writes a poetry of abiding generosity. His is an essential American voice."

Rodney Jones, author of *Imaginary Logic*

"Gary Fincke is a poet who brings a surefire eloquence and lively wit. His tour de force "The Extrapolation Dreams," meditating on family losses, shows to great effect his twin attributes of keen mind and large heart. We can be grateful for his artistry."

Colette Inez, author of *The Luba Poems*

"These poems draw from an intimacy of landscape, places of both unrest and clarity. Gary Fincke's poetry contains a rapt simplicity, humor, and grace. I love these poems."

Denise Duhamel, author of *Blowout*

"For Gary Fincke, knowledge leads us to the heart, to joy and sorrow—and the result is always a marvelous poetry that is both accessible and yet strange, both true and yet mysterious."

Andrew Hudgins, author of *A Clown at Midnight*

For Liz, Derek, Shannon, and Aaron, who have been a better family than I deserve, and in memory of my parents.

Thanks to Tom Bailey, Karla Kelsey, Glen Retief, Catherine Dent, and Silas Zobal for being great Writers Institute colleagues, to Codie Nevil Sauers for being there, to Kathy Dalton for always being willing to search, to Susquehanna University for trusting me, to the Degenstein Foundation and the Pennsylvania Council on the Arts for their support, to the editors who gave these poems a chance in books and magazines, and to all of my past and present workshop students who reaffirm that writing matters and keep me young.

CONTENTS

From WRITING LETTERS FOR THE BLIND (2003)

From BLOOD TIES (2002)

Prelude

Sometimes, when an audience
Is willing to listen to words
You once believed important,
When the half-filled room, formerly
A small chapel, reminds you
Of the usual affection
For language arranged briefly,
But carefully, upon a page,
You know how improbable
A poem's permanence might be.

Tonight, when you are to read
Your poems after a woman
Who performs in a beret
Jauntily angled and a scarf
Trailing fringe to her knees, you're
Embarrassed enough to ponder
Feigning illness, every word
You are about to read
As pretentious as her voice
Lifted at the close of each line
Already dense with inflections.

Finally, facing the pale
Expectations of the seated,
You leave your thin collection
Closed and begin with the story
Of your father, the janitor,
Unlocking, at midnight, the school
You attended years ago,
And walking to a closet
That opened, not to cleansers
And disinfectants, but a cake

Decorated with three lines,
In script, from your poem that
Remembers his long-closed
Bakery. From the cafeteria--
A knife, two forks and plates.
His invitation to eat.

The Light: New Poems

Assessing the Dead

When Gettysburg's dead, years buried,
were unearthed for removal
to national cemeteries, someone
was hired to separate Union
from Confederate, making certain
the loyal were rewarded, relying,
of course, upon jacket color,
but when difficult to tell,
shoe make and the quality
of underwear qualified
their wearers for graves
marked well-deserved.

My sister, twice, has studied
photographs to perfect display,
learning which necklace our mother
wore with her blue, Sunday-only
lace-trimmed dress, how, exactly,
our father's awards were arranged
for ceremony when he put on
his scoutmaster's uniform,
placing those reframed portraits
alongside both coffins like
mirrors or proof of love.

And now we've learned elephants
investigate the bones of their dead
by smell and touch, using the tips
of their trunks to caress what's left.
And yes, sometimes the young can
identify their parents,
lingering longer to inspect,
or, we like to imagine,
reflect. And whether saddened
or comforted by the ordeal
of recollection, they examine
the contours of the whitened skull.
Which is how reverie begins.
Then how it ends in turning away,
the necessary going on.

The Malignancy of Stars

Two hours to any sort of daylight,
yet a neighbor watches his wall-width screen.
A garbage truck makes just two stops along
our cul-de-sac street; the paper boy creeps
in his chuffing car. Beyond my neighbor's,
an ambulance has been parked an hour
at the seniors complex where three friends live.
I figure the odds and drop to the floor
for the sit-ups and pushups that follow
coffee. Consider this, I think. And that.
And I settle upon the belief in
the malignancy of stars, how bodies
may be selected from a great distance
for diseases. My oral surgeon, just
before my last appointment, has been felled
by a cancer so rare his specialist
had never seen one. Yesterday, I learned
his practice is closed. The receptionist
promised to send my records once I sign
a waiver—X-rays before and after
surgery, additional ones to probe
serious complications. When I walk
to the newspaper, I am close enough
to make out what's on, a woman speaking
from a bare stage, her gestures emphatic
and earnest. The camera finds women
in the audience whose faces are rapt
with belief in whatever has been said.
And though the power of any star but
ours is as implausible as faith,
the morning whispers attrition, the squalls
of constellations pass patiently low.

The Accomplishments of Birds

Ravens remember past relationships.
Crows recognize the individual
voices of birds of other species, and
lyrebirds, the males, can mimic any sound
they hear, from cameras to car alarms,
to attract quiet females for mating.
Such singing in Australia, but here,
for the third consecutive year, doves have
chosen the central crotch of our weeping
cherry, fluttering from the lawnmower
and car doors slammed in the nearby driveway.
For the third consecutive year, the nest
has collapsed in an early summer storm,
eggs strewn underneath the helpless shelter
of drooping branches. Persistent, those doves,
remarkable as the couple next door
who are paying for pregnancy, the wife
acknowledging each failure with something
I believe is akin to pride, her news,
just now, of the accomplishments of birds,
how studies have shown that a mother hen's
screeching can wake her chicks unhatched in eggs.

The Heart

Once, visiting Maine, I listened to my host
describe the haunch of moose she'd bartered
from a family after killing it with her car.
"All mine, by rights," she said, "but the father
dressed it out, fair trade," accelerating, then,
as exclamation point or hunter or simply
the lover of the woman sitting
behind us, a scientist she'd met
in Antarctica, the air inside
the speeding car so rich with intimacy
and story, change easily entered me.

In Minnesota, the hearts of moose
have faltered so often, too soon,
they are suffering a cluster
of early mortality. Now they are
wired, followed from a distance
by a veterinarian who explains
that when their hearts stop beating,
they send a text message to his phone:
"I'm dead at x and y coordinates,"
directing him so quickly to the downed,
he might decipher their clumsy hearts.

In space, we have discovered, the hearts
of astronauts become rounder.
In Pennsylvania, my sister, who
has examined the hearts of patients
in the commonplace of gravity,
has prepared herself for surgery.
The doctor is a friend, the anesthetist
a colleague. Already, she has been
monitored a dozen ways, a volunteer
for study, the details of her heart
to become averages or anomalies.

And last night, from Virginia, when
my vocabulary for encouragement
cried out and stumbled, I offered my sister
the weak consolation of my listening.
The muscle, she said, can regain what's
been lost. Just in case, I've updated my will.
Three hours, on average, this operation takes,
the intricacies that followed failing
to adhere to the moist walls of memory.

This morning, a waitress spread whipped cream
into a thick, valentine heart across
my son's banana-walnut pancakes.
Because, she said, a circle would never
make you think it's a heart, so unashamed
of sentiment, her heavy body turned
delicate in the sweetened air.

All this afternoon I am thankful for
the impossible distance to omniscience.
From across the room my wife's phone sings
its song of incoming text. In the altered
atmosphere, I believe our dependable,
dangerous hearts are becoming spheres.

There

In love with the light described
By the near-dead, my mother
Rallied her faltering faith.
She wrote to women her age
Who'd returned from heaven's gate,
Received an answer from one,
A woman whose heart had stopped
For nearly three minutes, who
Used words like "incredible,"
"Glorious," and "fantastic"
And finished with "Loving you
In the wondrous grace of God."

My mother slipped that letter
Into her Bible. She read
Those words so often the folds
Of pale blue stationery
Creased and split. "Don't you ever,
Ever, forget this," she said,
And lived another twelve years
Repeating, for ten of them,
Thomas Edison's last words,
The line he spoke reviving
From a coma, "It's very
Beautiful over there" while
She outlived her confidence
In a lush eternity
She would inhabit, feeling,
Like Mina, Edison's wife,
That "Over there" was the framed
Valley outside the window
He faced when he woke, the light
Splitting fall foliage something
Like the ordinary light
Of January, the sun
For her funeral failing
To spark the noon temperature

To zero, and yet, beside
Her grave, we squinted and raised
Our hands to comfort our eyes
In the bright, intrusive light.

The Drive-Thru Strip Club

Surely, an improbable business,
But here, on the road to Pittsburgh,
I enter Climax, where men watch women
Undress from the convenience of cars.
Like banking, like choosing breakfast
On a bun or briefly viewing
The just-dead from the driver's seat,
Here is sex tease timed like the scrub
And double rinse of a car wash,
The tires of the car positioned
Properly, gear shift in neutral,
So it slides forward at the pace
That's paid for, someone close behind
Waiting for the light to go green,
The door to lift like lingerie
In the hands of a new lover.

Though this morning Climax is closed
So I can park and open my door
Like a threat where women will enter
A double-locked door. Though, from the highway,
I'm as unrecognizable
As the masked, too early to pay
For arousal. Though a camera
Memorizes my car, but no one looks
At me where I'm standing like a woman
Late for work, a car already parked,
Forming the impatient traffic of need.
Though the heavy growl of speeding trucks
Sound so close I learn an excuse for walking.
To my car where I push the button
For start, hearing the interrupted song,
The one about women who no longer
Need men as intermediaries
In the era of violent desire.

Inexplicable

In the crowded airport, its escalator
steepened by my luggage and fatigue
and a nudge in the back, I remember
someone telling me that a student has sued
her college because it failed to account
for her allergies to escalators, tall
people and cactus, laughable until
my student claimed I towered over him,
that the offered chair in my office was set
so close to the cactus on a bookshelf
that he was afraid to sit straight, and when,
some days, I followed him down the stairs,
he was terrified I'd shove him from behind.

College counselor, I thought, good luck,
but a week ago, arms loaded with books,
I reevaluated those stairs,
calling up Michael Moyer, who shoved
a classmate down the thirteen wooden steps
of our elementary school, the ones
that ended in cement painted the silver
and blue of our school colors, the surface
slick across our mascot's sled-dog face.
Cradling seven volumes, I felt dressed
like a victim, recollecting how
spelling, geography, and arithmetic
flew from the hands of Paul Kelman before
he followed those textbooks down the steps
to concussion and a broken arm while
our teacher shouted, "You crazy boy, you!"

The week before, in Life, a psychiatrist
had explained play therapy, using a boy,
aged ten, who heaved clay against the life-sized
scrawled drawing of his brother, the body
chalked on the wall like the dead. The patient
declared he was happy now, and though not

exactly in love with that hated brother,
he'd stopped screaming, "I want to kill you!"
like Michael Moyer standing so still
at the top of the emptied staircase,
he could have been scribbled on the air.

That woman who sued claimed an allergy
to mauve, the pale purple shortening her breath.
My student drew pictures of stabbings
on the blue-lined white of notebook paper,
the victims unclear until two hall mates
recognized themselves by the added touch
of monograms, school counselor not half
of it then, dismissal immediate.
Though after he was expelled, I moved
that small cactus to a windowsill,
telling myself more light would make it thrive.
Within weeks it shriveled, inexplicable.
A secretary who examined it
proclaimed I'd overwatered, equating
full sunlight with insatiable thirst,
tending it so frequently I'd killed it.

The Danger of Yawning

Such long odds, certainly, for death from yawning,
But I've learned that over a thousand drivers
Per year die that way, distracted by the force
Of the ancient language for the need to sleep.

Who verifies such things? I wonder, thinking
Of the survivors testifying to cause.
And who am I, this afternoon, marveling
At the oddities of death, every victim
With a name I'm happy not to recognize.

Look, who doesn't yawn while driving the freeways
That hurry us long distance, the radio
Tuned to news of a war so lengthy it sounds
Like songs piped from the dropped ceilings of dentists.

Consider the size and timing that shutters
A driver's vision. Then imagine how once,
In Australia, a dwarf somersaulted
From a circus trampoline and plummeted,
Clown-costumed, into the incredible yawn
Of a hippopotamus, swallowed whole while
The audience applauded, then paused, waiting
With disbelief, like the parents of soldiers
Receiving a new, perfectly folded flag,
Impossibility laid precisely down
Upon the mother's quiet, unfurled hands.

Fraternity Brothers, 1970

Two years, Rich Cook had lived across the hall,
Giving me rides in his damaged car
Where we breathed the stink left behind
By a creek that flash-flooded hood high,
But this summer Cook was a soldier
In the Ohio Guard, and I was reading
The Victorians and Faulkner's novels
At Kent State where classes had resumed.
Since my second beer, I'd been posturing
As a near-miss survivor, and now Cook
Was drunk and angry and ready,
He said, to shoot me if history
Repeated itself. He carried
A pistol in that flooded Ford
I could see through the screen door
Where white moths were frantic to enter,
And he wondered out loud if I'd piss myself
If he decided to show-and-tell me
Just how cowardly I could be up close
With him and brother Bowers just back
From two tours and a pair of Purple Hearts,
Somebody who had survived
Hamburger Hill and nameless night patrols.
Cook asked if I was a Communist now
Or just some big-mouth asshole drinking
Beer with someone who was worth a shit,
And I was ready to renounce my years
Of second-hand graduate essays,
All of those sweet-sounding platitudes
Seeming as simple as pre-meal prayers
While I was composing apologies
And expecting both brothers to lay
A combat-tested beating upon me.
I could say the overhead kitchen light beamed
A Saint Paul moment of self-knowledge
And conversion, but what it did was
Flicker once when the refrigerator

Hummed into life just before Bowers
Said "Fuck the Guard" so matter-of-factly
I heard the period drop into place,
Ambushing one argument, at least,
In Youngstown where May was fishtailing
Into June, the three of us positioned
As if we still occupied our late-Sixties rooms,
A telephone hanging outside Cook's door,
The black receiver he had twice torn loose
Before sweeping into my room
After two a.m., both times silhouetted
Against the light, spitting, "It's for you."

The History of Hair

Once, pigeon droppings as bleach;
Once, a paste of houseflies to cure
Baldness; and once, with peroxide,
My long hair turned blond and orange
To celebrate the end of school
And amp my protest metaphor
With the language of hue and light.

For intervention or prophecy,
My father, days later, rubbed
His thumbs against my skull,
Promising hell-to-pay from
His brothers, the veterans.
My uncle with thin hair wished my head
Shaved like the French women who had
Fucked the Nazis. His thick-haired brother
Wanted to yank me bald because
I looked, he said, like shit.

From next door, his son dead that spring
In Vietnam, a neighbor cursed me
With his eyes, and what could I do
But walk outside, the following day,
After a barber had sheared me like
A sergeant, to push a mower
Across our lawn, a burst of starlings
Swirling up from our two maples
As I swept the perimeter,
Saying nothing about the art
Of applying pigeon droppings,
The time it took, collecting houseflies,
To concoct a miracle cure.
How, in ancient Rome, there were slaves
Assigned to capture and crush
Hundreds of bodies into
A restorative paste, each week
Renewing the salve, fingertips

Tentative on the scalp where
The persistence of flies might
Transubstantiate to hair because
Everyone agreed they rose
Spontaneously from the earth.

The Chernobyl Swallows

In April, near the anniversary
Of catastrophe, barn swallows returned,
Flying inside the exclusion zone to
Nest in the radioactive ruins.

Like disciples, the swaddled scientists
Marveled. The work crews, weeks later, toasted
The newly hatched, especially the fledged
With albino feathers after they soared

Like their siblings, devouring insects
With the ravenous hunger of swallows.
For months, the left-behind celebrated
How weak the worst was, and when the swallows,

No exceptions, flew southward, how feeble
Apocalypse could be. But come spring, not
One of the white-flecked birds returned, only
The ordinary nesting and spawning

Their own mutations. Families, by then,
Had moved back to where the world was quiet
And uncrowded, reclaiming rooms inside
The official radius of poison.

And through succeeding springs, no flight with white
Above them, just guards and squatters were left
To praise what they took for heroism,
Even if only among the swallows.

Recurrence

My sister names another experimental drug,
Describes one more miracle protocol, and
Reports our cousin's third operation, his flights
To a Texas hospital for the latest trial,
His prognosis three months, maybe less,
So thin, she says, his pants want to fall down,
His shirts hang like curtains, laying out
His cancer the way, every late August,
My mother held up what he'd outgrown,
What I'd grow into, dressing me for school
And church for a year, two if we were lucky,
Showing me why I needed to study,
Teaching me to control my pride and envy,
To overcome sloth, to manage gluttony, greed,
Anger and lust, launching into her sermon
On the seven sins that ended with the promise
That I'd thank her for the lesson of the threadbare,
The ill-fitting and the out of style, learning
What was good enough while she'd handed down
Her bad eyes, judgments, and chronic depression.
A third recurrence, my sister says, but still
Standing on his own two feet, wearing
Her hand me down language, adding
He's in our prayers and he's a fighter like
A litany, like I should say amen or sing
The Doxology before a recessional hymn of hope.
My sister, who learned to sew her own clothes,
Who wore homemade, but new, who needed
To perfect the careful cut and stitch because
She was older than every cousin, declares
"Our time will come" like some minister
For fatalism. She's at the window of the spare room
Where I've slept, saying the weather, so sunny
And mild, is heavenly while I try to ignore
The sewing machine, the half-finished skirt
And the thick file of patterns collected
In the good light I have to tear my eyes from.

Lie Still

For early photographs of babies,
The mothers hid under blankets plaid
And striped and single colored to hold
Their infants still. Photography asked
For time and quiet from their darlings
To be recognizable when framed.

In the portraits that survive, nothing
Disguises the shape of those women,
The way the cloth narrowed at their heads,
The taut geometry of their laps
Despite their care with preparation
For managing through cotton or wool.

Underneath, loose threads stroked their faces,
The mothers surely sweating throughout
The single, lengthy shot, laboring
In the darkness to aid the wonder
Of permanence, then holding their breath
To become inanimate for love.

The Mathematics of Ecstasy

This is the week I discover the pitch
Of the blue whale's songs is getting lower.
This is the week a neighbor, his wife dead
A month, swallows his car's exhaust after
He recycles glass and plastic as if
Sustaining a contract with the future.

This evening, mosquitoes swarm, their numbers
Swollen by September's record rain,
And I know that science has learned these pests
Choose mates who can harmonize perfectly
With them, duets enhancing the couplings
That bring some small equivalent of joy.

The shivering light of autumn assures
Their coming absence. The house of the dead,
Two doors down, lies dumbstruck. Such vanishing
Shadows us as we touch, fingers trailing
Along each other's chilled, bare arms, content
With the familiar. Our nerves, research proves,

Produce the greatest pleasure when stroked at
Four to five centimeters per second,
Though just now, I cannot mention this, not
Measuring distance and speed, ignoring
The mathematics of ecstasy,
Loving the beautiful discord of desire.

Six A.M., November

Her cries enhanced by the dorm wall echo,
The student sitting in the stairwell weeps.
A step above stands the boy who must have
Shown her that love is as perishable
As a thing stamped with shelf-life guarantees.
She raises a hand to her face. Without
Skipping a sob, she lets me climb. Wary
At public sorrow, the boy holds his stance.

She didn't lift her head, I say later,
Even when I paused like an eavesdropper,
And my friend says "aboulia" as if
I should recognize a strange, ancient word
For that tableau. A lifetime, he's studied
The obsolete and archaic, certain
There are words that fit so exactly to
Feeling they transcend the narratives for
Ambivalence, anxiety and angst.

Loss of volition, he says, loss of will,
Grinning as if he owns an antonym
To extract from obscurity, and yet
I am sure there are never enough words
To define my father, his knees ruined
To the threat of buckling, crawling backwards
Down the stairs to the flood-prone basement for
The years-old jars of my mother's preserves
That spoke one version of eternity.

Or my bald neighbor coughing up mucus
Beside the hybrid sapling he'd carried
To the hole dug for what he insisted
Would flourish faster than sumac, swelling
To shade my new house, the common use
Of urgency unfit for his latest
Experimental cancer therapy.
Or even light, this morning, an hour
Earlier and strange before six a.m.,

November, like the unexpected eye
Within a whirl of wind, nothing exact
For the certainty of early darkness,
The way it will precede Sunday's dinner,
How its voice will thump with the persistence
Of the bird that yesterday tried three times
To fly through the largest window that looks
Southward for solar heat, how it staggered
And yet steadied, lifted and disappeared.

The Light

The waiting room is half-full
of eyes damaged to specialized care,
those paired for post-visit rides,
marriages made by need,
whether shadows, sparkles, haze,
or the closing panels of darkness.

How often is light erased?

Inclusively.

Can you name the ways?

From diabetes, Robert Godfrey,
whose glasses were as dark
as each pair I wished for
in my daily dream of cool.
By macular degeneration
in the eyes of Emma Hemmerline,
who was always seated early,
last pew by the window that featured
Christ surrounded by a flock of doves.

Did you count ignorance and indifference?

Yes, my ineptitude with tools,
the refrain of no, not that way, no.
Her eyes said absence, their voices
Carrying like a stage whisper.

What about betrayal?

When promises are full eclipsed,
they can be examined,
but they will extinguish you.
Are there more? Have you seen them?

Glaucoma was Major Hartman, who dressed
in uniform each Sunday, never
using a white cane. Who took a stance
near the curb, looking at the vocal
while I waited for my father, who
found me so late, some days, the sidewalk
was free of men in white shirts and ties,
leaving Major Hartman to pivot
before trailing the staccato line
of his sister's reliable heels.

What about the sighted?

Eleven years ago, my neighbor
kept me awake for what, he said,
was rare and incredible.
At last, an hour past midnight,
Jupiter disappeared behind the moon.
Not again, he said, until 2026.
Not again, I said, in our lifetime.

What about the unseen?

From tumors.
From meningitis.
From birth defect.
From chemical burn.
From secrets well kept.

What about sixty years of the commonplace?

My father said glasses would disqualify me
from manhood, and yes, I nodded like a servant.

My father, proud of his eyesight, named birds only
at distances far enough to require my faith.

Oriole, he said, cardinal, goldfinch, speaking
as if he were the census taker for heaven.

And when I cried "sick," excusing myself from church,
he cited Saul transformed on the Damascus road,

as if my plummeting eyesight came precisely
from a God who might pick me for a change of name.

What about now?

The ophthalmologist, this morning,
confirms cataracts like appointments. .
Immature, he says, let them ripen,
what you have here so ordinary,
everyone who lives long enough
will have them. My wife, driving home,
says "the best you could hope for,"
meaning it's like remission,
daylight flooding my treated eyes.

What about then?

The storm of retreating light.
The body a burden.
My father's interrogation by silence,
His assumptions by grimace.
A year's work was brooding
And the determination to sleep.

What about now?

The world is a face of mouths.

Is this inexhaustible?

At eighty, my father,
refusing glasses, turned
into a curb, bending
an axle. At eighty-one,
he drove over a rock
that gashed his gas tank,
a trail following two miles

to his driveway. "Look,"
a neighbor said. "See?"
and walked my father
down the street, speaking
in his kindest voice.
Without repair, the car was
towed and sold. For nine years,
the driveway sat clear,
the garage abandoned
to the discarded.

From THE HISTORY OF PERMANENCE
(2011)

The Possibilities for Wings

How often have the customs of strangers
Silenced me into dreaming their beliefs.
In Java, for example, some people
Insist the souls of suicides return
In the bodies of crows, while in Scotland,
Souls of the lonely flee to butterflies.

In Pennsylvania? In this town where death
Belongs to those with names I've said, the souls
Of the ordinary are cries called out
And gone into an afternoon of rain,
Leaving me to wish winged things for the friend
Whose heart has failed, the friend who killed himself
In his meticulously sealed garage.

In my back yard? I'm talking to the friend
Who, like me, has sidestepped the terrible,
And even, from time to time, laughs aloud,
Neither of us, not yet, fluttering off
In moths or whatever we might predict
For our futures, the possible wings for
Depression, jealousy, the waste of hours.

Choose one? he asks, and I say the poorwill,
The only bird that hibernates, waking,
After months, to flight. Yes, he answers, good.
Overhead, just now, a small plane pierces
The air, and I imagine both of us
On board, becoming birds that seem to fly
Without love of anything but ourselves,
Shaping our fear against the summoned sky.

The Etymology of Angels

In Beloit, Wisconsin, a woman answers
The door in wings and halo, silver dress,
Welcomes me to her ten thousand angels
With "take your time and enjoy," fluttering
Like the authors of books who promise
Winged guardians are keeping us from harm.
The angel of the good deed, the angel
Of the safety net—half who answer polls
Believe, anxious as hospice visitors
Who avoid the terrible use of *next*.
Here is the theory of the angels who
Started a pilot program to transform
The world, two hundred fifty years renewed
Like a government grant. Here is the woman
Who encourages us to relax into
Our "sacred space" and wait for personal
Messages from heaven. Here is the handbook
For aspiring angels, how to provide,
How to facilitate, how to answer
The phone for the great CEO and transmit
The celestial e-mail to the faithful.
In the etymology of angels,
Diminishment sticks like a persistent gene
Until they sparkle like ten thousand pieces
Of kitsch, a woman's dress, the gaze of Azrail
Staring from the upstairs window as I leave,
One of his six billion eyes fixed on me.
And all along the rain swept interstate,
From the passenger side of each car that
Hisses by, Azrail mouthing the census
With one of his six billion tongues, adding
And subtracting while I form six billion
Questions of my own for the earnest angel
Who folds her pale hands, leans forward with knees
Together. This interview starts with Where
And When and Why, and this personal angel,
So professional, asks me to answer these

Myself because she's been employed and trained
By the great deflector, or perhaps that's what
Matters or else nothing matters at all.

The Serious Surprise of Sorrow

She's twelve, the girl who discovers a foot
Washed ashore in British Columbia,
Interviewed, she chatters, puzzled, amazed.

Attention is an awkward thing, she thinks,
And now she's been chosen as the witness
To the arrival of a miracle

Because two more feet, both left, like the one
She found, have landed on nearby beaches,
All of them wearing size 12 running shoes

Like a tiny cluster of rare cancer.
Surely they had mates, though left and right feet
Respond differently to the sea's currents,

According to the oceanographer
Who tracked, once, the paths of rubber ducks spilled
From a ship like a flotilla for joy.

Somewhere, then, the shoed right feet are floating
Toward another country, size 12 men
Targeted like unbribable judges.

Those feet will wash up on a thousand blogs;
Those feet will litter the crowded beaches
Of a million chat room conversations

Until time's incinerator turns them
To ash, becoming the urban legend
Of the wilderness that always concludes

With a girl who still believes that three men
Are limping somewhere on the prosthetics
For impossible chance, not already

Eaten by the grim mouths of the ocean,
That chosen girl growing into knowing
There is no limit to what we are asked

To accept, giving a personal name
To the serious surprise of sorrow,
Unable to stop scanning like those men

From our town's senior center who carry
Metal detectors to the nearby park,
Walking with stuttering steps like robins,

Their heads cocked a moment, then cocked again,
Their beaks passing over the unmown grass,
Listening for the soil's faintest sound.

After the Aberfan Disaster

On Oct. 21, 1966, in Wales, an 800 foot high "tip" of rock, coal, mud, and shale
collapsed, crushing an elementary school, killing 116 children and 5 teachers.

In this story, the assembled children
Have just sung "All Things Bright and Beautiful."
In this story, a survivor recalls
"In that silence you couldn't hear a bird,"
The slag thirty feet deep, a certainty.

In this story, the crushed children are called
By their parents. In this story, so few
Of them answer they become miracles,
The kind where ten lepers are cleansed, leaving
A colony of others to fester.

In this story, the children are smothered
By indifference, the company's and mine,
Because I am cowering from the draft,
Only college between me and combat.
That afternoon, I drive my father's car

One hundred miles per hour on a road
With a dozen intersections, and slow,
Trembling, into the sudden afterward
Of my brief, self-made miracle, thinking
What else proves I belong to the future?

Those children and their teachers are as dead
As two friends killed in cars. Some minister,
Days later, repeats, "In all things, design"
In a sermon I overhear, sounding
As if he's casting a blessing on rape.

A half mile from that service are slag heaps
High enough to take the light an hour
Early each evening. This story has me
Cautiously climbing each one with a friend
Soon to be blown apart in Vietnam.

Could there have been an alternate story
To the one I was breathing behind him?
So safely enrolled, who had I become
But a patient with purchased remission,
Reading about loss in expensive rooms?

Selflessness

In the animal kingdom, among fish,
one father carries all of the laid eggs
in his mouth, sixty-five day starvation
to make that flexible, deep mouth a womb.

Such sacrifice, spitting them out at last,
following that fast with the daily chores
of parenting: to guard them while they feed,
to take them back into his mouth like God.

Those babies need to grow before something
hungry finds them. They need a place to sleep
safe enough to wake again to feeding,
watched carefully by their selfless father.

He's a living prayer, that catfish who knows
each child as he opens his mouth for them.
Though every father has limits, and so
does this one, turning his back, one morning,

as they feed, swimming away while he still
knows them, before his children grow so large
he can't tell them from what he hungers for.
If he forgets to flee, he will eat them.

The Dead Girls

1

The girl who martyred her dolls, sending them
To heaven to wait for her arrival,
Sentenced them to stones or fire or the force
Of her hands to tear them, methods she'd learned
From the serious, dark nuns who taught her.

She would press a pillow over my face
To encourage sainthood. "Now," she would say,
Leaning down, and I'd let myself go limp
And lie quietly for her arrangements.

Her hands clasped like Mary's in the painting
Over her bed, she prayed for my body.
Sparingly, she sprinkled me with lotion.
Always, because she'd taught the proper way
To stare, my eyes were open when I died.

That summer, in the months before fourth grade,
Her uniforms waited in the closet
For September, her white communion dress
Beside them, declaring to St. Agnes,
Who watched from the sunlit, opposite wall.

In August, her mother ran a vacuum
Through the house, moving from the living room
Of St. Francis to the narrow hallway
Of Our Lady of Lourdes, and I stayed dead

Until the sound reached that girl's room, rising
To her mother's clenched roar of cleanliness,
Both of us keeping our feet off the floor,
Giving her a swipe of room to work, clearing
The way for temporary perfection.

2

The girl who loved to be touched in cemeteries,
Who said the dead reminded her to ecstasy,
Offered her body to my hands while I agreed,
Thanking the lost for their shadowed grove of headstones.

Always it was dark or nearly so, that girl shy
About her disrespect or nakedness, until,
At last, approaching cemeteries in weak light
Made me want to fuck above a thousand strangers.

One night, accidentally, the death of someone
Both of us knew, someone our age, meaning nineteen.
The violence of loss a lump underneath us
No matter which well-tended garden we entered.

Though frankly, we were exhausted by then, tired
Of each other's needs, and the dead could do nothing
Except talk among themselves about our absence,
Using the inaudible language of the earth.

3

The girl who died the following day
Is still talking in my car. She sits
Beside me, knees drawn up to her chin
Like a pouting child. Expectation
Is the only thing that will happen
Between us, the car's radio full
Of the British Invasion until
I follow her under the driveway's
Double floodlights to the house I will
Never be inside. "Next week," she says,
Before I drive past where she will die
In another boy's new car, the site
So often seen I notice nothing
But oncoming headlights, the bright ones
Under the influence of midnight,

The day she will die just now begun,
The radio switched to Marvin Gaye
And James Brown, the road so familiar
I can be careless with attention
As I speed toward the unexpected,
What weekends are for, story makers.

Things that Fall from the Sky

Seeds

Take one early evening. A father calls
His wife and children outside to witness
The eastern sky going bloody with clouds.
"What?" they say, transfixed, "What?" staring skyward
Until the rain swarms like sand, a brief storm
Of seeds that spreads them apart, their eyes closed
Under this brief anomaly of hail.

The after-light is so yellow it seems
To have traveled here from a jaundiced8star.
Before he can speak, the father must kneel
To examine that rain, his wonder turned
Watery, doubt taking his fingertips
Over their pinpricked skin to read the Braille
Of what might be born from a vocal rain.

A name for the first day of invasion
Wells up in him, a long vowel that leaves
Its breath on their faces. When they watch him
Like babies, that man smiles the first falsehood
Of devotion, afraid they already
Believe so much in these seeds, they'll swallow,
Certain that superstition will feed them.

Powder

> *In 1969, in South Carolina, nondairy creamer from
> the new Borden plant began to fall on a small town.*

1
The day became white and sweet
Like the air above a rolling pin

As a woman thins the dough
For chip-filled cookies. Children stood

Beside their mothers, their hands
Clutching toys they would not part with.

2
The weather cut the neighborhood
Into the shapes of families.

The cloud was soluble on tongues.
It surrounded each face like sound.

Already there were footprints
On sidewalks, a dream of shovels.

3
Those dusted by light took vows.
Suddenly, declarations of love,

The streets become hospitals.
Time was ending. A memory

Of old prophecies collected
In the eyes of everyone.

4
At last, the company's reassurance,
Though later, when the whitened bathed,

They stroked the film that had formed
Along their cheeks, their fingertips

Dizzy with the wonder of children
Touching the rouged faces of the dead.
Documents

> *In 1973 a set of papers that explained, with graphs and
> formulas, "normalized extinction" and the Davis-Greenstein
> mechanism of astrophysics, fell from a distance higher
> than a 300-foot radio transmission tower.*

When the paper fell from the sky, it looked
As if a briefcase had opened, a latch
Sprung loose among the clouds, spilling a set
Of documents, nothing in that story
To rush cameras right over, not when
There'd been a robbery and a fire, not when
The news desk smelled the late night stink of hoax.

But there was the detail of the tower,
How its height was cited, and documents
Aren't a rock format prank. Moreover,
This caller worked in radio, a sort
Of cousin to humor when he described
Formulas and graphs, suggesting a plot
Filled with spies or scientists dangerous
With political or religious hate.

A few lines then. A small item below
An ad for dishwashers, television
Running a gutted house and empty safe
As if its news were in summer reruns.
But after, when no one claimed those papers,
Chosen repeated itself like *amen*
As the last word of that witness' thoughts.

Prophecy, now, was physics, difficult
As a burning bush or exploding star.
And didn't "normalized extinction" sound
Like a careless spin on nuclear war?
He remembered the meteor legend,
How it explained the end of dinosaurs,
All things large starving in the dusty years
Of toxic darkness. Scholarship set in
Like the deep winter of apprehension.
Each night, before looking up, he wished for
The empty sky of the ordinary.

Meat

After meat fell from the sky,
After that shower ended
Like a cold tap twisted shut,
There were men who sampled it,
Cautiously chewing like kings.
Like mutton, one said, relieved,
Or venison, second choice,
Someone suggesting vultures
Had vomited together
From overhead; somebody,
At last, saying they were scraps
From God's table, calling up
The old words for mystery
That caught in the throat like bones.
The men who had eaten coughed
While wishes circulated
Like secrets pledged to silence.
For days, children examined
Their fathers for fur and claws.
Old wives were as tentative as
The child brides they had been, deep
In the nineteenth century
When transubstantiation
Was a bright, beautiful fact.

So it is with the strange.
A choir of analysts
Performed the old cantata
Of certainties until meat
Was people who had been ripped
To pieces by the sharp scythe
Of tornado, their parts swirled
Upward and returned as rain.
A family was missing.
Parables were passed through yards
Until streets of disciples
Formed a holy neighborhood.
A chattering of voices

Settled on porches, the words
So much the same they sounded
Like clouds of starlings rising.

Bodies

Begin with the one that famously
Landed on a San Diego car,
Dropping from a mid-air accident
Like a fantastically narrow storm.
Nothing can come from such plummeting
But disaster or the miracle
That needs snow drifts and touch downs precise
As ones that land softly on Mars, yet
The melodrama transfixes us
The way children, once, at matinees,
Were caught by serial cliffhangers
And spent a week believing rescue
As impossible as growing old.

That driver and her child were unharmed,
But afterward, she had a habit
Of glancing up like a forecaster,
Though it's rare, anyone looking up
For the descent of bodies, rarer
To believe they're falling from a cloud.
It takes the height that turns us breathless,
A thousand feet or more to make us
Think "sky" like one morning when distance
Throttled our breath while suited bodies
Plunged like drops of a passing shower
That pockmark the dust of current drought.

And I, for once, agreed on something
With my sad, conservative neighbors,
Desiring a sect of people dead,
Their lives snuffed by gene anomaly.
The body of Christ, the blood of Christ—
The chorus of communion became

The password into our side for war.
It drummed in the inner ear like pulse,
And I dreamed myself marching to plant
The first flag of a lifetime, tending
It each morning as if cloth might die
And declare me criminal and cruel
In the common carelessness of peace.

Meat-Eaters

In B-films, the carnivorous plants
Are always huge. They swallow anyone
Who wanders near, a single knot of vines

Tugging a victim into the dark maw
Of horror, not discriminating
At all, as if eating were accident,

As if they were human. The real killers?
Some work together like the field
Of sundews, in England, that ate,

Within hours, millions of butterflies,
One true story that illustrates
The collective achievement of plants.

But working alone, selectivity
Is what matters. The Venus flytrap
Measures its meals so it doesn't

Squander the down time of digestion
Upon the undersized. The jaw seals
Slowly, the spaces between its teeth

Allowing the escape of small insects.
So size-selective, its mouth, the young
Can flee, the tiny can skitter away,

Not through mercy, but efficiency,
What's necessary for survival
When rooted in the earth's poorest soil.

Specificity

For Len Roberts

Cause of death unknown. Had never been fatally ill before.
Death Certificate, 1880s

Until I was twelve, *worn out*
and *God's will* were the reasons
my relatives died, my mother
speaking like a doctor, citing
visual evidence
or unknowable matters
of faith as if each were
a diagnosis of disease.

In the King James edition
of medicine, the self-help
my grandmother relied on,
there was the finality
of dropsy, the chronic palsies,
what Jesus cured, like leprosy
and possession, the devil
imbedded in the flesh like ticks.

Before she was born? People died
from convulsions and fever,
from infancy, age and tissick,
the collective name for killers
that came with coughs, as frequent
as smallpox and grip of the guts,
what the dying did, at last,
when their digestion failed.

Approximation. Guesswork.
Less of that now, the x-ray
showing the shadow that will kill us,
the blood sample spilling numbers
that count us out, each tremor

specific, a thousand names
exactly right, pinpointing
each particular way to die.

Amyloidosis, for instance,
how one friend, this week, has gone.
And now, after memorial,
after an hour of tributes
by poets who traveled hours
to eulogize, I sit with my wife
who orders a glass of Chambord
for a small, expensive pleasure

in a well-decorated room,
the possibility of happiness
surprising us in the way
hummingbirds do, stuck in the air,
just now, outside this window,
attracted to the joy of sweetness
despite the clear foreshadowing
of their tiny, sprinting hearts.

From REVIVING THE DEAD
(2011)

Telling the Bees

In old England, after a death, family members
went to the nearest beehive to tell the bees.

My father, at eighty-nine, abandoned
His yard to hired help and neglect. He drew
His bedroom drapes as if he were closing
That theater like a bankrupt business.

He opened, one morning, those year-closed drapes
And saw, astonished, a wasp nest grown huge
Under the eaves, something to watch instead
Of the television he could not hear.

He followed that window's feature each day,
The silent movie of work, the mute slap
Of small bodies on glass, and though it is
A custom to which I give no credence,

And though they're not even the bees of myth,
I work my way among the Rose of Sharon
Planted, years ago, as fence, and offer
My reason for visiting, come to choose

Photographs as keepsakes after the death
I announce to the busy air like someone
Superstitious enough to think the words
I use must be understood by the deaf.

For Good

He's dead and gone, and yet you read
That a man in Serbia has
Driven a stake into the grave
Of Slobodan Milosevic,
As if superstition has not
Been domesticated to flags
And flowers, as if you might walk
To the gravesites of those you hate
In order to spike the soil
And repeat, three times, "For good."
As if you might haul that stake home
In the trunk of your car, something
To keep in the garage among
The garden tools, the grave's earth dried
And caked upon its brittle point.
In early March, you hammer it
Into the ground among a bed
Of perennials; throughout April,
You examine the earth, and when
Every bud reappears you weep
And carry that stake inside where
There's a place for it by your bed,
Your hand reaching for it each time
The darkness speaks its dialect
Of shame, holding its point over
Your heart to coerce a symbol,
The Milosevic of yourself
As adamant as April while
You rehearse like a citizen
Of a tiny theocracy
Where consolation can be held
Like a stark, sacred affliction.

Dust

Missing the ride that ended in wreckage,
A friend's mother dead where I would have sat,
I remembered his dashboard St. Christopher,
The rosary beads that draped it as double
Insurance for loss. I spent an evening
Reading about relics, splinters of ark
And cross, the shrouds of the saintly, holy bits
And pieces that signified paradises
Made possible by faith and ignorance,
Circumstance, chance, all of them, yesterday,
Reduced to wishes under the Imax dome
Where the Hubble photographs demonstrated
The enormity of dust while my friend
Strained to find representation for faith.
So near his lost comfort, the heavens became
A billion suns where surely someone worships
While elsewhere someone suffers the terror
Of understanding. A voice recited,
In light-year language, the vocabulary
For endlessness, yet my friend threw his head back
To absorb the Pillars of Creation,
Those famous nebulae, and I listened,
Beside him, to the theory of dark matter,
Eighty per cent of the universe ascribed
To the utterly transparent darkness
Of the unobservable, hearing him
Murmur the brief acquiescence of amen,
The lenses of our eyes enhanced to the scope
Of gods who, knowing the unaccounted for,
Turn their flimsy backs to the expanding dust.

Evaluation

Overhearing, in a bar, a student
Declare my poems conservative, line
By syllabic line, I sat myself small.
Art is such a pretty thing, she prattled,
And more important, unfathomable.
Nothing could be truer than mystery.
Writers had used commas for centuries.
Enough of that, and enough of letters
In upper case, time arranged by verb tense.
Conventional spelling? Why so stuffy?
And forget about syntax that travels
The worn path of clarity. When nouns fail,
There are coinages; when verbs seem frail, drop
Hyphens between two like beautiful yokes.

There were mixed drinks scattered nearby, the kind
That feature flavored vodka, two liqueurs,
And small splashes of tropical juices
Sparkling in sugary combinations.
The bartender, because she's an artist,
Makes them only once. The bowl-sized glasses
Confirmed it, the color otherworldly
As the cloudless heavens above Xyrgyst,
The seventh planet from a pair of suns.
Across from me a man nursed beer in which
A plum slice swam like an exotic fish,
His mug an aquarium to admire,
And I heard pentameter spit loudly,
Narrative shouted like a blasphemy,
Regardless of suffering or who loves
Alone, the reliably ordered heart
Voicing its rhythmic, conventional needs.

Scattering

From six to ten pounds, our cremains
Will weigh, the visible fragments
White or gray, the largest pieces
Ground to sand-size for discretion
And the ease of our scattering.

Not comforting, this summary,
But better, pre-need, than the one
Describing decomposition
By traditional burial.

Better yet, post-burning options
Carry romance for the living—
Etched keepsake urns, ash-speckled cards,
Jewelry that carries cremains
Near the wrists, the throat and the heart.

Carry ceremony, as well—
Scatterings at sea, in meadows,
Off cliffs or the small balconies
Of the deads' high-rise apartments,

Because height, most often, is craved—
From airplanes, from helicopters
And hot-air balloons, even from
The raised barrel of a shotgun
To ensure a high arc of dust.

And lately, fireworks, with music,
Those ashes blown into rainbows
To ooohs and aaahs from the living,
Bringing to mind what's new, the launch

Into space, the years-long orbit
Until small meteors of ash
Plummet again into burning.
And now there are those who will pay
For lift-off to the moon and Mars,

The beautiful, infinite ride
Beyond solar system borders,
Escaping, they convince themselves,
The great scenario of ash,

How the Earth, in a billion years,
Will become a planet of dust;
How, finally, it will spiral
Into the huge, expanding sun,
Which, while dying, will scatter Earth

As if it needed to render
All of our cremains to swirling
In eternal memorial,
Perfecting grief, at last, because

There's never enough preserving,
Never enough remembering
As we fling those we love in wide,
Then wider arcs, as if distance
Can photograph the dead, create

An image we're able to see
When we're alone, concentrating
On some speck of sky as we breathe
The heavenly dust of the loved.

Translating the Hawk

For three days, the hawk perches on our roof's peak, at the west end where it overlooks my wife and me on our deck, from where it can swoop down and reach us with its claws and beak before we leave our chairs. Each day are hours of absence ended by flight we follow because we sit outside and wait as if the sky were television, the hawk a program filmed exclusively for us. We feel changed beneath it, August curling shut, brittle with heat. We celebrate the guest we do not speak to, whatever it sees in us staying secret as death. And though we cannot name it, narrowing by color and size, we believe it a male who returns because we wait, the hawk on the house a yoke of used time we gladly shoulder, the hawk making us rise before dawn, our doors left open all night because we want our emerging to be silent, just the screen's soft shuffle outward and back, the hawk, three times, exactly where we left him, his evenings a story he will tell us when we learn to translate the silence the way we have learned to interpret God, what he might be saying from another world which can only be reached through flight.

From **THE FIRE LANDSCAPE**
(2008)

The Anomaly Museum

My mother believed in the prophecy
Of metaphors, ignoring the omens
Of our literal street where husbands worked
And their wives kept house. The anomalous,
She insisted, foretold the promises
Of the body, citing the child just born
With fur, the woman with a forehead horn,
And most telling, the boy whose head ballooned
To show us salvation's fortunate sign.

"To make room," she said. "To accommodate
His beautiful, enormous soul," meaning
For me to consider my thoughts, turning
My headaches into hope and fear, making
Wonder from misery so rare, the way
A reader might take these syllabic lines
As one more expression of "look at me,"
Each word a disguise for deformity
Like the airbrushed nudes in the night museum
Of magazines I toured during high school.

Then, while my mother's heart turned commonplace
With disease, I entered classrooms to face
The exhibits for terrible fortune:
The boy with Thalidomide stumps, the boy
Bent breathless by tumor, the girl whose lungs
Thickened to failure. Kevin and Rob. Greer.
I can recollect their names thirty years
Or more since I passed their symbolic selves
In the hall of occasional horror.

All along, my cousins were carrying
Their latent, faulty genes toward the three sons
Who would show that flaw in their sluggish brains,
Those boys calling up the face of that child
Who disappeared inside the great swelling
Of rare luck, the impossible size meant

To console us who need only foresee
The common routes to death, the stroke, this week,
That froze one side of a friend, his voice gone
To the slurred vowels of my cousins' boys.

The truth is that yesterday my friend still
Inhabited such a possible face
I looked everywhere he wasn't. And now,
In the museum I visit by myself,
I examine the bleak pornography
Of anomaly, attentive to how
The plates of one childish skull expanded
Until they burst open like a flower,
So impossible there is not one thing
To do but think of the boy as blossom,
Disregarding the ordinary parts
Of him until they go unremembered
As the busy shapes of nearby tourists.

Black Veils

I learned the verse where God demanded hats,
Found the reference to veils. For hundreds
Of Sundays, the women around me were
Covered by the lace-like, black strands of tulle.

I saw that men can show their face to God,
Learned that faith surrounds the heart like cotton.
Without it I would hear my pulse, go mad.
The dead were delivered at once or damned.

The veils were raised by hymns; they fell for prayer,
Fluttered through the long words of the pastor
As if something frail and invisible
Was beating its wings against the fine threads.

The dark veils were as serious as smoke.
They whispered the soft language of the dead—
Mrs. Shuker, Miss Swope—I knew the names
Like the books of the Bible, Genesis

To Revelation. When I tried one on,
I sensed the dim humility of hope.
When I examined myself in mirrors,
The clothes I wore needed to be undone.

The Sorrows

Whatever the Sunday, the sorrows kept the women
       in the kitchen,
My cousins and their mothers, my grandmother, her sister,
       all of them
Foraging through the nerves for pain. They sighed and rustled
       and one would
Name her sorrows to cue sympathy's murmurs, the first
       offerings
Of possible cures: three eggs for chills and fever,
       the benefits
Of mint and pepper, boneset, sage, and crocus tea.
       Nothing they
Needed came over-the-counter or through prescriptions
       not bearing
A promise from God, who blessed the home remedies
       handed down
From the lost villages of Germany for the aunt
       with dizzy spells,
For the uncle with the steady pain of private swelling;
       for passed blood,
For discharge and the sweet streak from the shoulder.
       In the pantry,
Among pickled beets and stewed tomatoes--the dark,
       honeyed liquids;
The vinegar and molasses sipped from tablespoons
       for sorrows
So regular they spoke of them as laundry to be smoothed
       by the great iron
Of faith which set creases worthy of paradise. And there,
       when only
A hum came clear, they might have been speaking from clouds
       like the dead,
But what mattered when the room went dark was the voices
       reaching into
The lamp-lit living room of men who listened then, watching
       the doorway

And nodding at the nostrums offered by the tongues
      of the unseen
As if the sorrows were soothed by the lost dialect
      of the soul
Which whispered to the enormous ache of the imminent.

The Horns of Guy Lombardo

Because I am ten years old and unashamed,
Because I've played the trombone for a year
And can read songs from a book of standards,
I walk off our porch to play Auld Lang Syne
At midnight to my family's applause.

My parents must know that a year from now
I will refuse to play for our neighbors,
But this is how we spend the first two minutes
Of 1956, the year before
I worried about sex and God's absence.

I am as confident as the flood light
That illuminates the black, simple notes
And casts shadows so dark on the driveway
I can see the slide extend and retract
Like the sluggish tongue of an ancient frog.

My father is about to be thirty-eight,
His nails, even on off-days, black with work.
That evening, he knows his bakery
Will fail, groceries filling with cheap bread
And cake mixes easy enough for fools.

My mother's body is beginning to sag
With the weight of her collapsing thyroid
And the heavy numbers of blood pressure,
But she smiles and begins to sing the words
Like someone who expects to recover.

The snow, I imagine, is softening
My tone, making me sound as mellow as
The horns of Guy Lombardo, what the rest
Of the world kisses along to unless
They have stumbled outside at midnight, close
Enough to catch my song, hearing something
Like resolutions flung into the air.

False Dawn

My father shook me from sleep to say "Look,"
Directing me east toward a cone of light.
I thought he meant me to know the H-bomb
Had finally fallen, that our campground
Was fortunate to be a hundred miles
From Pittsburgh, even farther from New York,
The city I guessed was first to explode.
I stared at the end of the world, waiting
For him to explain what would follow, and
Because there was no moon, that glow faded
To the first question I managed, thinking
Radiation, "How far away was that?"
"How far away is the sun?" he answered,
Sounding so symbolic I expected
To be dead that day until he added,
"Now you can say you've seen something special."
At five a.m. I lay awake, telling
Myself there was a baseball game of time
Until sunrise, one inning already
Ended, the second started by strikeout.
"It's space debris," he murmured in the dark,
And I imagined the small particles
Of Earth drifting toward somebody who knew,
Like my father, what false dawn was, how dust
Could glow when aligned in the moonless night.
School would soon begin in Pittsburgh, still there,
And Miss Bell would elaborate, for sure,
On the canals of Mars, what she had taught
My sister the year before, how Martians
Had been so smart their incredible work
Could be seen from millions of miles away,
Yet they had vanished like the dinosaurs.

White Gloves

Going out meant church, my mother,
Like a surgeon, slipping on white gloves
At the door. They said she was ready;
They said get in the car, sit in back,
And remember, keep the window up.

She held a tissue to the handles
And knobs between our house and our pew.
She wore them once and washed them; she owned
A second, identical pair,
Three ridges along the back that matched

The two pair in boxes she'd wear new
For Easter or Christmas or weddings
That requested extended hands.
White gloves, she said, were like glasses,
What she needed to see past herself.

The President's beautiful wife wore
White gloves like lipstick, her newsreel hands
Bleached by public expectation,
But after Dallas, my mother
Entered her Sundays without them.

She prayed with her fingers touching
Until only old women were white
To the wrists, and she died, three pair
In the drawer of her last things, two pair
Waiting in boxes like the souls

Of the unborn, so patient, so long,
They were lamps left on when the day
Enters through windows, light unnoticed
Until evening when we're surprised
And say to ourselves, remember.

Like Ours

Ninety students and three nuns died in a school fire
In Chicago on December 1, 1958.

For days after the fire, we talked about
Our Lady of the Angels school, how boys
And girls like us had died in their classrooms.

Miss Anderson said that school, like ours, was
A chimney, and we needed, each of us,
To pay attention now, lips zipped and sealed.

They had one unreachable fire escape,
Wooden walls and floors like ours, years of wax
Building rectangular plains of candles.

She said the common corridor we used
Would be impossible with smoke, and we
Listened, so quiet, already like ghosts.

Their windows, she told us, were tall, their sills,
Like ours, twenty-five feet from the pavement,
Our fall the same as Catholic children

Whose parents paid to keep them safe from schools
Like ours, where nuns and priests were characters
In jokes that featured discipline or sex.

"Readiness," she said. "Remember." And when
The bell slapped us, a ruler to the wrist,
We lurched up as we did for pledge and prayer.

Outside, rain was freezing, weather so bad
The alarm seemed real. Like ours, their school day
Was almost over. Like ours, their weekend
Was beginning. "Calmly," she said. "Now go."
The sleet slicked the fire escape's iron steps
And our uncovered heads until eighteen

Of us, silently descending, broke loose
From the brick wall, our bodies flung against
A railing that rescued us like firemen.

"Hurry now," she said, "go down," and we did,
Assembling like a choir, everybody
Singing the same chorus that morning, safe

Until we climbed the main stairs to our room
From which, like theirs, no exit existed
But the long, luminous stride into air.

The 1918 House

My father, whose limp is a stutter,
Says he was born in the epidemic,
The early days, when people survived
Like expected because it was just flu.

In May, he tells me, the cases were
Three day fevers. By June, he says, the flu
Had moved to where it always summers,
Far from the warm weather of families.

My father, who shuffles like those who
Are stared at by children, accepts my hand
For surfaces other than sidewalks
To examine every place where he's lived.

In September, he tells me, symptoms
Meant death--the coughing of blood, the blue face,
The darkening of feet that said "soon"
In the common language for conclusion.

The lungs, he says, went soggy with blood,
The people drowned for days. The newly born,
He murmurs, were passed over like sons
Of Jews, God's mercy on our infant breath.

My father, who refuses a cane,
Touches a wall he built in a yard owned
By strangers, pausing on his way to
The beginning, the house where, in the year

Of the Spanish flu, he was first-born
And no one died, where his parents survived
To see themselves chosen, praising God
And good fortune and their lifetimes of work.

On both sides, he says, are the houses
Of victims, sons who enlisted for war,

And he pauses, the porch so different
I have to read the number to prove it.

How winter blessed us, he says, ending
That horror, driving us inside to love.
He asks me to knock on the white door;
He says these people will invite us in.

The Pause in the Plummet for Prayer

They'd plunged thousands of feet, crash-certain, and now,
Miles above the Pacific, a passenger
Walked the aisle like a stewardess. Let us pray,
She said, and believers, those passengers did,
Filling the unexplainable nine minutes
Of frail stability with supplication.
That plane scribbled like a toddler on the sky
While every one of them felt saved, we're told, Flight
Two Sixty-one's miracle joining the best
Stories that begin, "Did you know?" passed forward
By the bucket brigade of word-of-mouth, and
Emptied, sent back by the living, retraced from
Here to there to witnesses who cannot speak.

No matter the disaster stories we hear
And repeat, a marvel of wishes spreads from
Our words--healings, sightings, the necessary
Resurrections growing like the hybrid tree
We planted--in seven years, the tallest thing
On our street; in seven more so enormous
We took it down, and yet it drives a thousand
Descendants from roots spread the length of our yard.
Our neighbors walk out to a field of saplings
Sprung up like gifts from the magi of desire.
This morning, standing among them, we marvel
At the force of rebirth, how, if everything
Returned, we would stand in the darkness of awe.

From STANDING AROUND THE HEART
(2005)

Standing around the Heart

We stood, in health class, around the cow's heart
Miss Hutchings unwrapped on her desk. Inside
And out, she said, we need to know ourselves,
Halving that heart to show us auricles,
Ventricles, valves, the wall well-built or else.
Her fingers found where arteries begin.
She pressed the ends of veins. Richard Turner,
Whose father's heart had halted, examined
His hands. Anne Cole, whose father had revived
To cut hair at the mall, stepped back, turning
From the entry to the steer's aorta,
The four chambers we were required to know.
While we watched, Miss Hutchings unwrapped the hearts
Of chickens and turkeys, the hearts of swine
And sheep, arranged them by size on the thick,
Brown sack, leaving a space, we knew, for ours.
We took our pulses. We listened by way
Of her stethoscopes, to each other, boy
To boy, girl to girl, because of the chance
We'd touch. Those butcher hearts warmed while I dreamed
Of pressing my ear to the rhythmic heart
Of Stephanie Romig, whose breasts, so far,
Had brushed me one time while dancing. And then
Miss Hutchings recited the quart total
Of our blood, the distance it must travel,
Leaving and returning, all of the names
For the necessary routes it followed,
Ending with capillaries so close
To the surface, we could nearly reach them
With our lips and tongues, rushing the blood to
Each of the sensitive sources for joy.

The Eternal Language of the Hands

The surgeon Celsus, at the time of Christ,
Said the right hand should operate
On the left eye, the left hand should invade
The right. He meant the interns to practice
From the weak side like switch hitters,
An old strategy which makes us smile,
But the smug health of the moment
Turns a page in the book of longing:
I looked left, then right, at the pictures
My father showed me: the husband, the wife,
Through five generations which ended
In German scrawled unintelligibly
Across the back. I was young enough
To believe, because he had lived
With grandparents who spoke privately
In German, he would translate the three pairs
Born somewhere other than Pittsburgh.
I expected a second language to
Enter me like the left-handed layup
I practiced each day, but he said German
Was forbidden like taking the Lord's name
In vain, that he'd shaken off Kraut and Hun
And Heine, slurs I'd never hear because
We'd changed. He might as well have tried,
Like some, swallowing a child's raw heart
For beauty and love. Consider
How many cataracts Celsus removed,
Inserting his needles, nudging them
Off-center like wind-blown grit. Left, then
Right-handed, thousands of years before
The surgeries we wait for. My father
The baker rolled sandwich buns with both hands
At once, circles so tight you couldn't tell
Which had been formed from the left or right.
Like Celsus removing clouds and teaching
Those miracles to disciples
In the eternal language of the hands.

The Buchinger Limbs

In the year I wrote small, everything
I knew could be copied on a page
If I practiced until I mastered
The perfect penmanship to succeed.
A corner for school, thin lines along
The bottom where lust and pleasure spoke.
Inch of family, a column of friends,
The short sentences of school and work.
I was a tenth grade wonder, shrinking
Myself to stumps of ink, but my aunt
Told me tales of Matthew Buchinger,
The man with flippers for arms and legs
Who wrote seven Psalms and The Lord's Prayer
As the curls of his self-portrait hair,
Reducing those articles of faith
To miracles of calligraphy.
So tiny, she said, each of those words.
Think of holding the pen with a fin,
Using that grip for the common sense
Of achievement. On the news, reports
Of thalidomide. In Germany,
Where her father had come from, cases
Of the newborn with Buchinger limbs.
Look, she told me, so many deformed
We will soon not notice the dreadful.
If you can learn anything at all,
The smallest words will drive you blind.

The Uses of Rain

We sat, in geography, for nine weeks
With water, a marking period of rain.
We followed the dittoed diagrams
Of water's efficient recycling--
Precipitation, evaporation,
All the clouds we memorized for exams:
Cirrus, cumulus, the great thunderheads
Like the ones Mr. Sanderson called us
To watch at the windows. Snow, he told us,
Was nature's cheap ice cream, more air in drifts
Than water. A barometer, he said,
Could thrive inside an injured knee. But he
Made us read the names for irrigation,
How crop rotation and the geometry
Of plowing could safety-net the earth.
He taught the proper times for lawn sprinklers,
The folly of building in the flood plain,
And we remembered the time tables
For tides, the value of delta, wetlands,
And the extraordinary ecosystem
Of the ocean. And though we conserved
For extra credit, though we catalogued
Our care, we took our test, turned it in,
And listened, books closed, to Mr. Sanderson
Tell us the story of the crested bustard,
Whose desire is triggered by the sound of rain.
"Because it lives in the desert," he explained,
"Its courtship dance must be timed just right."
He held our stack of tests to his chest
And walked among our rows. "In zoos," he said,
"In captivity, those birds begin to dance
When they hear a keeper's hose. They prance
To the simple sound of cleaning, believing
That rain will water the luck of their children."

Sweet Things

All the way through doughnuts I sang along
With the radio because they were the last
Sweet things I laid my hands on before my shift
Was over. My father was busy with icing,
Blending color with different degrees of sugar,
And then he had an hour of pastries to fill
With custard and fruit to compete with the rolls
On television that cakewalked to the oven.
In the bakery, time raised bread and browned it.
Time hand-rolled sandwich buns, carried pies
And coffee cakes to cool on countertops,
None of them strutting off their pans after
I stepped into snow, inhaling with the joy
I thought I'd earned before dawn, driving
The station wagon four miles to where
My mother was drinking sugared coffee
And eating zwieback she'd brought home stale
The night before. I heard news, weather,
And the drive-time deejay say Bobby Vee,
Connie Francis, or some sound-alike
For success because it was time for
The reasonable world to test itself.
And I left that car on the plowed street
So I could say the hell with shoveling
Our driveway with the snow still falling,
Exhaling with my mother before she closed
The door on the Chevy still warm and steered
It back to the bakery in the changing light
To sell to men finishing one shift
Or starting another at the mill,
Each carrying a bag of sweet things
Into the ordinary ends of morning.

Bringing Back the Bones

I read about the men who maim themselves,
Who amputate fingers and toes and arms:
The man who practiced on pork shoulders and
Put, finally, the shotgun to his leg;
The man who crushed his leg, set it afire;
The multiple cases of men who lay
Their legs across the railroad tracks and wait
As if the world has insufficient loss.
I remember two friends who lost both legs
In cars, others who gave up toes and feet
To diabetes. I want to write them
Whole, bringing back the bones, though my father,
Each time I visit, reminds me my words
Are no different than bread he baked, the cakes
He iced by hand, squeezing out the sweet script
Of birthday names. He shows me, this trip,
The school bus full of old books and papers,
Tells me he's driving them to Aspinwall
For dollars by the ton. We stand, later,
In the leveled lot of the razed bakery.
He scuffs one mark for the workbench, one more
For the mixer, nods at my shoes and waits
Where the dough would rise while I toe the earth
And tell him my tale of the wooden legs
On the child mummy unwrapped in Egypt,
The carbon-dating that said those legs were
Centuries younger than her bones, someone
Opening the grave and fitting those legs,
Someone forming sized feet from reeds and mud.

Anniversary

We learn, today, a girl who attended
Our wedding has been murdered. Thirty years,
We say, guessing her age—eleven? twelve?—
From the old photographs that help us tell.

We read the articles from three papers—
Cord-strangled, the saw taken to her limbs—
One picture, then another, something like
A legend beginning, something like hell.

Just home with her fiance, our daughter
Looks at our young selves. The summer evening
Reaches into our kitchen; she helps us
Name the naturally dead, chanting a spell

For her mother's white gown, what my daughter
Will wear, this gift she tries on, beginning
To enter her story, raising the sleeves
To her face, drawing them closer to smell.

The Weaknesses of the Mouth

There were punishments for the weaknesses
Of the mouth. Two uncles had killed themselves
With salt and fatty meat; an aunt had slaughtered
Herself with sugar. "Each of them knew,"
My mother said, but I was growing
Into the bone-stunting of tobacco
And candy's pimples, "God's way," according
To my mother, who warned me about
The pack of pink gum I found and chewed,
That there were dope dealers who seeded
Desire with good fortune, waiting for
The next day of need, that gum, alone,
Enough to empty my mouth of teeth.
I stopped talking, then, about the warm dance
Of tongue and lips, the moistures driven
By the heart. The first beer I swallowed
Poured warm from three bottles I found
In the half-razed house where old rubbers
Told me there were willing girls nearby.
I had such weakness I finished the fourth
Long-opened bottle, stepped, minutes later,
Through the lost heat register's empty hole
And stuck at my shoulders instead of
Tumbling to cellar's glass and nails.
It was the last polio summer,
Seven years until my first cold beer,
Reversing the Pharaoh dream, famine first,
Refusal urging my mouth to open.

The History of Silk

In seventh grade, when we were alone for
An afternoon, no chance of being caught,
Silk was what we sought in our sisters' rooms.
It was enough to hold silk and name girls
Who were slipping off the slick things we touched:
Pajamas, panties, lace-trimmed slips with straps
Designed to be nudged by passionate hands.
Three or four together in those bedrooms,
We turned alike, drawing silk things over
Our skin like fingertips, lifting our shirts,
Opening our pants in dark unisons
Of desire that made us refold those things
Exactly, replacing them in order
Until the afternoon one of us slid
That silk over his head to bring himself
Closer to pleasure, and he did, though none
Of us would touch or talk to him, the words
For his body disappeared long before
We knew the history of silk, the way
Taming turned the silkworms from tan to white.
The way, defenseless, but unharmed, they stopped
Trying to escape. The way, become moths,
They didn't fly, how they mated and died,
Without once opening their damp, pale wings.

Headcheese, Liverwurst, a List of Loaves

Our refrigerator
Opened to liverwurst,
Headcheese, a list of loaves:
Luncheon and Luxury;
Olive, Old-Fashioned, and
The great alliteration
Of Peppered and Pimento.
We eat, my father said,
One hundred million cans
A year, justifying
Our Spam. Three per second,
He figured, and we sat
For sandwiches he cooked
Because I refused them cold.
"You just don't know what's good,"
He said, and I agreed,
Refusing altogether
Potted Meat Food Product,
Looking it up, lately,
To find "tripe, suet, beef hearts,"
Memorize the mystery
Of "partially defatted
Beef fatty tissue," to tell
My father, who's laid out
Cold cuts of celebration
For his restored heart, shaking
His head at snouts and stomachs,
All the meat byproducts
I can recall while we spread
Mustard or mayonnaise,
Add pickles and onions
To the short stack of squares
And circles between thick rye
With seeds. And I listen
To my father repeat
"This is eating" before
Our first bites, smiling while

We swallow extenders
And gelatins, relish
The joy of fat and spice.

Coughing through the Brambles

Some days the asthma wakes me early,
Makes me walk through the underwater dark
And trust my footing to prescriptions
While I find the shallow end of wheezing.
So quiet, this illness, so unlike
The bark of the common cold, the great whoops
Of the cough more serious that killed
One classmate the winter the whooping crane
Stood extinct, almost, on the front page
Of our Weekly Readers. We watched slides
Of condors and grizzlies and pale fish
We were supposed to care for, and even now
I watch for Harvey Walker, the sun
An hour away, because his spirit
Might choose to retrace itself, search for
An arrangement of houses and yards
And debris which calls up our childhood,
The dwarf shape of fear whose messages
Stay simple as those folded inside mittens.
For asthma, once, you swallowed spider webs;
For whooping cough, some parents would push
Their children through blackberry brambles,
Those stems which arced to thrust themselves
Back into the ground like living hoops,
Listening to the terrible thrusts
Of air through the constricted hoops of throats.
It was like the laying on of hands
For tumors and tuberculosis;
It was the faith and prayer of my parents
Who passed me through the brambles of eternal
Damnation, expecting answers the way
Some men listen for responses to
Radio waves they transmit to outer space.
The year Harvey Walker died, I read
A story about the first broadcasts
Reflecting off the edge of the universe
And returning for rebroadcasting.

"O, Holy Night," the radios played,
By Professor Fessenden, 1906,
And then Bible verses from St. Luke,
Stutters of stations working toward
The cacophony of perpetual
Retransmission of a billion broadcasts.
And I might pass all of the past's coughing
Through the brambles which run the border
Of the lot I live on, three times each,
One thrust exactly like the others
In distance and direction until
The heavenly white magic takes hold.
And I might lay my healer's hands
On the vulnerable spots of those
I love, trusting the medicinal
Power of faith, but I've weaned myself
From the vanity of prayer, believing
Enough voices are rocketing toward
The imagined edge of the universe,
So many supplications seeking
The thin, improbable antenna,
The unlikely decoding, and then,
So far to return, so many requests,
The everlasting shower of granted
Wishes soaking the astonished
Descendants of the faithful and
The faithless, flooding both with bitterness
And joy, and drowning the need to believe.

Miss Hartung Teaches Us the Importance of Fruit

The banana is a herb, she said, but
The Koran claims it's the forbidden fruit.
The orange is a berry. Grapefruit is new.
On Fridays, when we opened our lunches,
She lectured on our apples, plums, and grapes.

A President, she said, after hogging
Cherries, died; a French king, over anxious,
Bit the prickly skin of a pineapple
And shredded his greedy lips. Remember,
She said, tomatoes and olives are fruit;

Eat your salads and think of them as sweet.
She brought papayas, mangoes, kiwi, figs;
She taught the origin of the lemon
And the domestication of the lime.
She said there are 5000 kinds of pears,

Doctors who prescribe them like booster shots.
Pick them early, she warned us, or they go
Gritty; let them ripen in your kitchens
Or the cells inside them will turn to stone.
Listen, children, she said in June, the peach

Preserves the body. The Spanish brought them,
And even the Indians learned to love that fruit.
And why not, don't all of us know the way
To everlasting life? Don't we all have
An instinct for the perfect gift from God.

Johnny Weismuller Learns the Tarzan Yell

For public appearances, for the crowds
Who expected perfection, he managed,
Take after take, to mimic the sound
The studio had built for an ape-child.
Practice was like swimming all those laps
In the pool, building his breath again
To fill the audio needs of Tarzan:
Camel's bleat, hyena howl played backwards--
He couldn't admit to plucked violin,
A soprano's high C added, one
After the other, to his own best roar,
His champion's howl so much a common cry
The audience wouldn't think "explorer caught
In quicksand," "hunter surrounded by spears,"
Not Tarzan loud in the natural world
Where the hybrid voice develops into
The great arpeggio of beast and man.

The History of SAC

1952
In the hospital, in the enormous ward,
Forty-eight iron lungs were breathing for
The tri-state's victims. Nurses paused to murmur
Near each disembodied head, the room
A theater of whispers, the film obscure.
My aunt, their supervisor, held my hand.
I breathed in and out through my sterile mask
And thought of steam irons at the dry cleaners,
My father's two suits tagged and returned
Like pigeons. The smell of trichloroethylene,
How it dizzied, how it followed us
For a half block of store fronts. On runways,
At that moment, thousands of bombers
Were idling in case Truman or Stalin
Decided to end the world. In the sky,
To our north, a shift of squadrons hung
Like the mobile over the face of the boy
In the row to my right, second lung.

1972
We drove to a runway's end, the great
Passenger planes lifting six minutes apart,
Banking and turning toward selected cities
Like missiles. We parked and faced the squat cliff
Like the disembarked; the sky became
A belly so heavy it had to fall.
That evening, you clutched yourself by the stove,
The front, right burner coiled red under
A sauce pan poised for boiling. Wait a while,
You said, let's see, and turned the water to LOW.
After the coils went dark, you said
"Yes, again" and disappeared to dress.
The plates and silverware lay bare three days.
A nurse walked the aisles among the isolettes,
So many babies breathing so easily,

I listened for the heavy approach
Of apprehension, the water in the pan
Transformed to air, the kitchen turned metallic,
The stove sitting ready as a SAC bomber,
Idling on LOW until you handed me
Our son and dialed it slowly down to OFF.

1992
In the AIDS unit, we walk with my sister,
Who has a grant, hundreds of thousands
Of dollars, to study the attitudes
In care for these lethal patients, the poor,
Twenty to a side. I keep to the center,
Curse myself like I do when I refuse
The sturdy rails at overlooks, dilettante
Of the blood. I think of yours in that instant
Which fixes us to eternity,
That son old enough to contract disease
From his ward approach to sex, and when we
Reboard at America's newest airport,
Enough runways to handle the SACs
Of a hundred nations, my childless sister
Says, "We're going global," sweeping her hand
As if she means to peel off the horizon.

In Films, the Army Ants are Always Intelligent

Water and fire again, we think, watching
Natives dig a trench, lug the gasoline
To its banks. It's the white man's solution,
Some land owner protecting investments,
All those years of cheap labor just lately
Paying off. Ants, after all, are ants, but
Understandably, he's a bit nervous
When his workers chant, fumble with magic
In a pouch. Savages, he's learned, always
Sense when the absentee gods should be called.

And we might wonder, while the cameras pan
The rain forest for troops, if these things rest,
If there's a day along the Amazon
When you could sleep off hard work or a drunk
In safety. And why there's still a jungle;
And why these ants, a million years of them,
Haven't eaten every square inch of green.
There's never a natural predator;
There's only the good sense of travel north
So climate can negotiate with them.

All we're taught, at last, are the miles of them,
That their sign language ripples front to back,
Reaching the billionth soldier correctly.
Remember that schoolroom game, the one where
Miss Harshman whispered a message into
Janey's ear? She turned and whispered those words
To Billy who whispered to Sally and
Thirty seats later you recited them
To laughter that blossomed from the first row?

Think of yourself as sluggard in the rear.
For days you've had nothing to eat, the ground
You're covering stripped clean ten thousand ranks
Before you. Well, somebody has to starve,
You might conclude, improvisational

In the tropics. But then you feel the word,
Sense *plantation, panic, picnic for all.*
So there's sacrifice ahead; there's something
To those parables, you see, when your turn
Finally comes: The early waves were burnt;
The first leaf rafts were sunk; and you're certain,
Dancing before battle, that the water
And fire are gone, that the natives have fled
Or been shot in the back by the owner.
So he's on his own now, self-destructive,
Or maybe he has dynamite, something
Apocalyptic. On the other side
Of the moat there is feasting. All you have
To do is cross, stepping from one body
To another, to cultivated land.

Dragging the Forest

After the First Aid Meet, after our patrol
Revived Mike Hofaker, who played the victim,
My father, the Scoutmaster, settled us down
With our scores for bringing back the heart and lungs.
Correctly, we'd stopped bleeding, and perfectly,
We'd treated shock. We'd made splints from newspapers
And neckerchiefs, eased them around our problem's
Broken bones and carried Mike Hofaker through
The hall by makeshift stretcher to prove safety
For the judge who'd scored us second, total time.

"You think you could save someone?" my father asked,
Driving me home along the Allegheny.
I looked at the water, but my father said,
"Up there," nodding toward the steep hill of forest
Where, he started telling me, he'd spread his arms
And walked in a line one hundred Boy Scouts wide.
"We were flanked by men," he said, "who repeated
`Fingers touching.' The boy had been lost two days.
We hiked up, moved sideways, walked down. We sidestepped
And started up again before three boys screamed."

"The lost boy, of course, was dead," my father said.
"He was tied naked to a tree, eleven
Copies of the out-of-date *Sun Telegraphs*
Folded up inside his bag like an address."
I thought my father meant me to be careful.
From where we were driving the river was black,
The woods thin enough to take the sun's last light.
Scores came on the radio. The teams were Pitt,
Army, Syracuse, Notre Dame. From bottom
To top, the width of the woods went to shadow.

From WRITING LETTERS FOR THE BLIND
(2003)

The Busy Darkness

What the Optometrist Said

The eyes facing forward means predator,
Along the sides of the head declares prey.
Better here? Worse? Any difference at all?
To find our way in darkness, we must have
Six times more light than panthers. To make out
Danger, we need ten times more light than toads.
Try these. They'll fit a face as thin as yours.

The rhinoceros sees so terribly
It charges large rocks, occasional trees.
You can stop squinting now. It's a habit
You've formed through neglect. Don't you see yourself?
What do you think? Your eyes aren't corrected?
That there's too little light? That you can't see
What's approaching before it gets too close?

Writing Letters for the Blind

For fifteen cents, or twenty, in the script
I'd mastered from Miss Hartung, I wrote
Saturday letters for Bill Nelson, who
Sat blind with a white cane beside his chair.
He loved the letters in return, the lines
Scratched out in pencil or blue ball-point ink.
This is Gary writing, he had me say,
And women, often, when they wrote, added
Postscripts that began *for your eyes only*
As if I wouldn't read their words aloud.
Such a dear, they repeated. *God bless you.*
We should all have such a generous son.
When one woman had her daughter write me,
She folded that page inside her letter
So Bill Nelson, holding the envelope,
Smiled and said, "It's a good one, two pages."
Straight out, that girl said her mother wanted

Us to meet, that the slope of my letters
And my way of crossing *ts* showed I was
A boy to be trusted when we were grown.
Before he paid me in nickels and dimes,
From a change purse open on the table,
Bill Nelson measured every coin by touch,
A test, for sure, because everybody
Knew the blind heard better than the sighted,
And I passed for months, not stealing, until
A woman mailed a dollar postscripted
For me. It lay so quietly, so thin
On the table I read, "The five dollars
Are for Gary," giving myself a raise.
Would Bill Nelson believe I was worth it?
Would he consider his coins and add them
Higher in my hand? In fact, I hoped so,
Because I wouldn't steal, taking nothing
From the blind but what I thought I deserved.

The Era of the Vari-Vue

"He can see shadows," my father told me,
"Bright light and pitch dark," as if Bill Nelson
Had time-traveled from the Bible's first day.
From a front seat, squinting, I could copy
My teacher's chalked words; from my desk I could
Recognize friends' faces four rows away.
The spring I was failing that blackboard test
And the exam of the curveball, I thought
Everybody saw with the soft focus
Of myopia, hunched down to pages.

In the first, fad years of the Vari-Vue,
My father brought home plastic-ribbed pictures
Of Plymouth Landing and Christ on the Cross.
The proper distance, he said, the right tilt
Of the head until I wig-wagged Pilgrims
Ashore; the eyes of Jesus to heaven;
And signed, bobbing my head, a small, slightly
Blurred, Declaration of Independence.

Dog-at-the-hydrant. Cow-over-the-moon.
Finally, I wore glasses. By the time
I mastered contact lenses, I could shift
Nixon's eyes in the White House windows, could
Surface my children's skulls and nod my wife
To bones, flicking her forward, fast or slow,
Like mutoscope women you could undress,
Once, for a nickel. Now, for quarters, men
Can lock up in booths to watch looped films, choose
Sound-suffused channels on the porn network,
Sighed syllables of acquiescence flung
Like dots on this page I'm holding tonight,
In the gallery of unimportance,
Trusting they will leap up as holograms.

I'm staring at a near-wash of purple,
Coaxing "halved spheres" or "peeled fruit" off paper.
I'm deciphering instructions, learning
The sure ways to 3-D without glasses,
Pulling the page haze-close, one simple step
To "deep sight," the *trompe l'oeil* of computers
If we posture ourselves like the near-blind.

You enter the page, the inventor claims,
And I imagine the third dimension
Of pornography, toxins surfacing
In lakes, futures embossed by tainted blood.
I call each of my chattering, clear-lensed
Children to these pictures, say "hold this close
And stare," prodding them to levitate balls
And fruit, say "pear" and "globe" as if these were
Rorschach blots for the willingness to see.

Remedies

The Sioux believed in opening the eyes
To the dust of bezoar stones they found
In the bodies of buffalo and deer.

The British, once, believed in the power
Of baking a black cat's head to powder
For blowing in the eyes three times a day.

And some of the nearsighted, more squeamish,
Have worn gold earrings, trusting the bright loops
To recall the radiance of vision.

Pushing the Black Thread

> Hagop Sandaldjian, the world's only microminiature
> sculptor, was described as "a very calm man."

Last night I couldn't thread a needle.
I took it under three kinds of light;
I licked that thread; I ran it between
My fingers and thought luck, finally,
Would pull it through while I remembered
The man who sculpted between heartbeats,
How he kept his hand steady enough
To carve Snow White and the Seven Dwarves,
Red Riding Hood, and Cinderella,
Each sculpture so tiny he placed them
In the slim eyes of sewing needles.

What he carved can't be seen unaided.
For all I knew, his lost Mickey Mouse
Deflected my thread that threatened art.
"May all your dreams come true," that sculptor
Etched along one hair, but he used lint
For Presidents, dust motes for the Pope,
And I pressed my chest, at last, against
A high-backed chair, studied my pulse for
The instant of greatest calm, pushing
The black thread, failing, pushing again,
Listening and listening with light.

Not the Worst

Not the worst, the doctor says, matching

Me to his patient list. Not the worst,
Sounding so rehearsed I imagine
The patient who only sees shadows,
Welcoming, whore-like, whatever moves.

In the country of perfect vision,
Would anyone record what was seen?
And gone into exile, would those eyes
Wear themselves dry with excessive use?

Look. Gaze. Watch. Stare. When every edge turns
To haze, when persistent fog compares
Our hope to the hell of indistinct,
We listen for the breath of beauty,
The custodian of clarity,
Sweeping, unable to keep us clean.

Better, Better, Worse, Better

Last night I woke and saw nothing and knew
It was my Bill Nelson dream, the one where
He makes change in the dark, handling each coin
In his black purse until he's satisfied
Which ones are proper. I imagine him
Cheating himself; I imagine keeping
His quarters and lying about the blind,
How they mistake coins the way I misread,
With my fractioned vision, the brief rebus
Of road signs, the puzzle of passersby.

This evening, I trust my sight to the eyes
Of my neighbor, the optometrist, who
Listens as I say, *"Our Hearts Keep Singing,"*
Describing the album by the Braillettes,
Three blind women beaming good attitude
And bright hope from their cover photograph.
"It's on *Heart Warming Records,"* I finish,
Taking air puffs between blinks to confirm
It's not glaucoma that's sucking my sight.

I stammer, "Better, better, worse, better."
I hear diopters, thickness, the great curve
Of this year's inadequate correction.
The doctor hums the ceiling tunes. Follow
The light, he croons. Now ignore it. Although
I want to say "How?", half-expecting him
To switch it off, smiling in the darkness
At optometrist humor. "Worry you?"
He'd say. "Got you to thinking?", plummeting
The room to black, waiting for my answers,
My optimistic eyes still dilating,
Whether or not I'll be sadly clever
With compensatory, heartfelt singing.

How the Optometrist Encouraged Calm

During panic, when your mouth dries,
Breathe out until the count of six.
Breathe in until four. Count slowly.
One, two, three . . . more slowly than that.

Try to remember it's just your brain
Mimicking the symptoms you dread:
Breathlessness. Dizziness. The chest
Going tight, tingling through the hands.

Better yet, recognize your fear
Is only anticipation.
Fight it with facts. Be specific.
Darkness is danger not yet here.

The Fathers I Could See from my Room

The father who lifted sample cases from his car,
The father who carried a briefcase full of grief,
The father who tallied the pros and cons of spending—
What did they do in those offices where nothing
Was built, no customers to please? What changed
By their leaving early, by their sickness, retirement,
Or death? We had moved to where one father mowed
His lawn in white shirt and tie; we'd left behind
The street of fathers who entered factories
And mills at seven or three or eleven.
I knew what they did because they detailed it drunk
On weekends when the world could wait for the things
It wanted. When Sputnik circled the planet,
When the Communists made something we couldn't buy,
We watched, on the news, the melancholy arc
Of America's latest failed rocket. The fathers
Who wore suits kept doing the work that makes nothing,
And one of them, while I slept over with his son,
Brought betrayal home at midnight, what we shouldn't hear
About faithlessness. Below us, in the driveway,
His Lincoln looked like it spent all day in an office,
Like a woman had starched and ironed it. That father
Let his wife talk herself into leaving. My friend
Propped himself so long on his elbows I wanted
Something like mumbles to squeeze under the door,
Sounds so simple they could turn into regret.

What Color Did

When disease strikes, it is because the colors of the body's elements have
fallen out of balance – Dinshash Ghadiali, inventor of the Spectro-Chrome

Color mattered. My father held out shirts
And ties like a ring-bearer and waited
For my mother to match. And while she was
Deciding, he offered her socks and pants,
The two sport coats he owned in brown and blue.
In the early days of the pastel shirt
For men, my father seemed too old for choice,
The simple era of the white shirt gone,
This time for good, so much depending on
Color, it was almost medicinal,
Curing shyness, uncertainty and fear.

Not the first time for that. *Normalating,*
As Dinshash put it, was what color did—
In other words, therapy for the sick.
See, he advertised, the elements most
Common in us are linked to hues: The red
Of hydrogen, the blue of oxygen,
Carbon's stoplight yellow, nitrogen's green.
See, he explained, shining filtered light bulbs
On the skin above his patient's organs,
Here is the way to brighten or dim them,
Regulating the rainbow in ourselves.

Color mattered. My father faltered when
Patterns came to his shirts, pinstripes and plaids,
Madras and paisley and fields of flowers
That made a perfect match impossible.
Close enough, my mother would say, holding
Those shirts and ties to the natural light.
Close enough, yet my father turned tight-lipped
In public from her doubt, unbalanced through
Sundays until he pulled on the full green
Of his uniform for work, sweeping up
After children who wore clothes like models.

Not the first time for that. Dependable—
What the boss called him as he aligned desks,
Arranged chalk by color while my mother,
At last, purchased "The Healing Scarf," praising
Its silk and its rainbows dyed to contain
Every shade needed for recovery.
She studied its guide to color's power.
She learned the locations for pain. She wore
The scarf on her skull to balance her brain's
Intricate rainbow, and trusted the shade
Of x-rays, the felt color of chemo.

Then my mother died, her rainbow of clothes
Packed and donated. My father recalled
Three combinations, washing and ironing
The plain shirts--blue, beige, and gray--laying them
Out with the ties and socks on my sister's
Unused bed, repeating them fourteen times
Through a year of Sundays and twice during
The six Wednesdays of Lent, rotating through
Good Friday and Christmas and Thanksgiving,
Funerals and weddings, as many as
Twenty times a year then, the simple shades
What he knew of color, dressing himself
Three ways for God, one for work, until he
Became all silence, unbalanced, and dark.

Marking the Body

My doctor, a woman, knows how shyness
Shrinks men gone vulnerable in the groin.
She waits while they unbutton or unzip,
Turns from me this morning, giving me time
To excuse myself with a just-learned story:

Behind a curtain, once, women would mark
A female doll exactly where they hurt:
Just below the breasts, for instance, covered
By the doll's uplifted arm, they charcoaled
A cross; low in the belly they scratched an X.

My doctor knows that history; she says
My male doll has Xs over the lungs,
Cross-hatches on the throat, skipping the spot
For this morning's mark, the way I've never
Been this slow to undress for her instruments.

My doctor, who knows when eternity
Begins to form far out in the future's
Ocean, covers her hands in the latex
Of discretion, reaches for me, and says,
"The feet of those draperied women were bound."

My doctor, who would have passed that Barbie
To the discreet hands of a physician,
Examines me like a familiar doll.
She breathes high on my naked thighs, that air
The first that fails to stir the stiffening blood.

She pivots, strips her gloves, and I follow
The intimate lines of her breasts and hips
To the softness of myself, fixed until
She turns, finally, in the last moment
When we both are deciding what's arriving.

124

The Early History of the Submarine

In the handed-down writings of Pliny.
In Herodotus; in Aristotle.
In DaVinci, who fears The Flood's return
And sketches his own elaborate plans.
In failures. In the men who construct them
And drown. In Cornelis Drebbel, who sinks
And resurfaces, confident as God.
In his passengers. In King James the First,
Who demands a ride. In closing that hatch.
In sliding under the surface, the king
Watching the hull, listening to those walls
For the limits of greased leather and wood.
In Drebbel saying five, ten, fifteen feet.
In their settling and the king exhaling.
In the oars they pull together. In talk,
Finally, of windows and speed and air.
In Drebbel, at last, slowing his breathing
To give the king a larger share. In joy.
In surfacing with wishes he's prepared.

Otherwise Healthy

Twice this week, choosing from near the bottom
Of the list of phrases I rarely use,
I've murmured "otherwise healthy" as if
It explained the history of allergies.
The foot doctor who lives nearby has died
From a bee sting despite his antidote.
The five in my family, slouched on the deck
From summer dinner, shake our heads, listen
To my daughter tell us, a second time,
She swallowed liqueur speckled with gold dust,
And her throat shut tight as if it wanted
Nothing more. Though after she gasped and wheezed,
After her friends begged the bar for doctors,
She saw strangers stand to say "what?" and "how?"
Like magician's children, the evening's whim
Deciding, then, to soundlessly inhale.
"I could have died a metaphor," she says,
"The woman with an allergy to gold,"
And we list the odd possibilities
Of "sunshine" and "moonlight," "the songs we love,"
How we turned up our favorite music
As we walked outside on this clear day, just
Before sunset, daring the light and dark.

The Plagues in Order

For Children's Day, for the church pageant
Performed by the primary classes
Taught by the Misses Shuker and Swope,
We were the plagues in order, changing
Costumes while Moses spoke, returning
Ten times to taunt the unbelievers.

In crimson sheathes, we were the river
Turned blood. Masked and hopping, we were frogs.
And when we heard, crawling and flapping
As lice and flies, the *ohs* of adults
From the pews of Etna's Lutheran Church,
We knew a day's praise was seething for
The holy revenge of our costumes.

Like cattle, then, we went to all fours,
Lowing and listening to Miss Swope,
Who spoke for God from the balcony,
Promising the plagues to everyone
Who hardened his heart like a Pharaoh.
Like Egyptian cattle, we buckled
And fell to the side-sprawl of dying.

Look, there was more. We all wore white hoods
Circled by the red of boils, flung
Brown rice as hail before we chattered
Like locusts and swarmed off to black-sheet
Our bodies, waiting for Miss Shuker
To switch the church to darkness we made
Darker, shivering like just-freed souls.

And when we caught the collective hush,
The first-born among us dropped and died,
The rest solemn despite being blessed
By the lottery of birth, standing
To the sides like two halves of a sea,
Walking in wide pairs from front to back
To the street as if we expected
Our chastened families to follow.

Birds-of-Paradise

After surgeries, after one knee
And then the other were scraped and cleaned
And made comfortable like the dying,

I swung myself on crutches, then limped,
Then slow-walked near normally until
This next breakdown of cartilage and bone.

Tonight, my father says, "Now you know,"
Phrasing satisfaction or despair
With his old rhythms for speed and bluntness.

Together, we slide and shuffle down
His stairs, do the awful one-step
To the music of irreparable.

For all it matters, for comedy,
I call out my turning radius
In a short expletive of self-pity,

Watch my father manage the minute
He needs to rise from a chair and lurch
To his collection of canes by the door.

"Some mornings," he says, "I wake thinking
My legs are amputated, yet there,
That I've been revised like your best poems,

My knees small hinges that bend just air,"
And I believe, in that moment's rhyme,
That he's prepared for me by rehearsing,

That before mobility's rapture,
We'll redesign ourselves by omission,
Taking away all the common parts

By which we are compared, becoming
Birds-of-paradise, which, because the legs
From the first specimens sent to Europe

Were removed for easier shipping,
Were thought to perpetually fly
And live by eating the dew from heaven.

How's it Going?

In the bilingual comic book,
Extending his hand and smiling,
A boy fills the over head bubble
With "How is it going with you?"
Employing the stiffened English
Of classrooms. What do we expect
The grinning, cartoon Chinese girl
To answer? "Fine. And how are you?"
"Greetings, I am pleased to meet you."
Not this time, her copy altered
By the stroked white of cover-up,
Fresh type that mimics the font size
And style, giving her the message:
"Fuck you, you fucking cocksuckers,"
So convincingly, one student,
I'm told, used that sentence to greet
Her new foreign-exchange family,
Shaking father's hand as she spoke.
"How's it going?" he'd said to her,
Tense as I was, blurting, first day
On the job, "How's it going, Joe,"
To the college president who
Would fire me, a few years later,
"Because, guy, you're not happy here."
How difficult is our learning?
I'd stuttered that phrase, at fifteen,
To Sandy Stephenson, who laughed,
Repeated it and laughed again
Outside the tenth grade home room where
I'd staked myself to ask her out.

I remember all those failures
Because that translation story
Ends with the girl's apology,
The host-mother embracing her
As if obscenity blessed them,
But this morning, coming back to

Classes, I noticed a colleague
In her darkened office, and said,
"How's it going?" before I took
Three more steps and saw the answer
In lost weight, pallor, the silk scarf
Tied tight around her skull. She forced
The brief, tentative laugh of grief,
Kept her expletives to herself,
And I thought, a moment, about
Sharing that altered scene with her,
Giving her the chance to answer
"Fuck you, you fucking cocksucker,"
Translating the cancer, holding
Out her hand or pulling it back
Because, didn't I see, she was
Hosting the foreigner, not me?

The Magpie Evening: A Prayer

When magpies die, each of the living swoops down
and pecks, one by one, in an accepted order.

He coaxed my car to start, the boy who's killed himself.
He twisted a cable, performed CPR on
The carburetor while my three children shivered
Through the unanswerable questions about stalled.
He chose shotgun, full in the face, so no one stepped
Into the cold, blowing on his hands, to fix him.
Let him rest now, the minister says. Let this be,
Repeating himself to four brothers, five sisters,
All of them my neighbors until they grew and left.
Let us pray. Let us manage what we need to say.
Let this house with its three hand-made additions be
Large enough for the one day of necessity.
Let evening empty each room to ceremony
Chosen by the remaining nine. Let the awful,
Forecasted weather hold off in East Ohio
Until each of them, oldest to youngest, has passed.
Let their thirty-seven children scatter into
The squabbling of the everyday, and let them break
This creeping chain of cars into the fanning out
Toward anger and selfishness and the need to eat
At any of the thousand tables they will pass.
Let them wait. Let them correctly choose the right turn
Or the left, this entrance ramp, that exit, the last
Confusing fork before the familiar driveway
Three hundred miles and more from these bleak thunderheads.
Let them regather into the chairs exactly
Matched to their numbers, blessing the bountiful or
The meager with voices that soar toward renewal.
Let them have mercy on themselves. Let my children,
Grown now, be repairing my faults with forgiveness.

From BLOOD TIES
(2002)

The Tentative Steps of the Obese

Lately, the news has been following
The man who's been lying in bed,
Too fat to rise, for fifteen years.
Now he's lighter by a hundred pounds,
Standing in his doorway, but he can't
Come out today, says, "I'm not ready,"
Though he may just be exhausted,
Puzzled that anyone would care about
The tentative steps of the obese.

Someone says, "He ate like a sweeper,"
And I title him *Fat Man Hoovering*,
Remember what I've learned about
The invention of the vacuum cleaner,
How the concept came to Cecil Booth,
Who put his lips to carpets and sucked
Dust to the ecstatic proof of choking.

Booth's hotel room had residue
For a million tests, maybe a year's
Worth of feasting for the dust mites
He didn't see, those trenchermen
Of his carpet working nonstop
At feeding, growing invisibly fat;
And as the news drives elsewhere,
The dog looks up and listens and goes
To the door to growl at the unheard,
And all I'm believing, suddenly,
Is our personal range of senses
Has shrunk. That we could see those
Dust mites once. That we noticed what
Swarmed and fed. That we nearsighted
Ourselves to forget them, forget what
Towers over us, huge as the newscast's
Fat man, who has five hundred pounds to go.

And I'm following the dog's loud lead.
And I'm thinking, let all of these tenants
Step outside to the eyes of someone.
Let them blink a shy astonishment
At the lenses that admit them. And let
Them be changed and go on changing
And float like dust mites, their bodies
So light in death they rise from our
Carpets like souls, ascending, perhaps,
To ceilings or settling again on our beds,
Gone to some paradise of lost skin that
Tumbles from the nerve ends of the living.

The Extrapolation Dreams

*Villard de Honnecourt, a French architect, wanted to
use the perpetual-motion machine he designed to power
"an angel whose finger turns always toward the sun."*

Brownian Movement

The blizzard was ether.
A few minutes walking
and all the superficial
parts of me were prepped
for surgery. I was
hazy to be home, to leave
my share of the town's
teenagers stuck inside
the weather of stranded,
weekend school. There's
staying awake, I'd thought,
living in the gym with
students; there's pain
horizontal snow won't numb.
And what was a mile
in a Buffalo whiteout?
Fifteen minutes, twenty.
New York wasn't some
Jack London snowbound
deathtrap. I told myself
two thousand steps would
end the cold. I dreamed
counting could put up
panels, that four walls
and a roof could be built
by hundreds, heat to follow.
But that storm witched me
zigzag to two thousand
and nowhere but the blank
deep of the street until
the dark smother of freeze

held its pillow over my legs.
Another thousand, I said,
for sure. And there were
other houses; I didn't need
my wife and children.
After three thousand strides
I could live anywhere
indoors. Surely I'd reach
a porch that the drifts
hadn't erased. Surely
some family would open
a side door and gather,
astonished, in the hallway,
to see who they'd saved,
who'd returned, prodigal,
from the swine of that storm.

Coriolis Force

Today, the silver-anniversary reunion book in the mail, autobiographies by my classmates that begin with Lyle Anderson, a surgeon who's living in Harrisburg, who has a green belt and a son in diapers. And Susan Arend, whom I don't remember, complains that working full time keeps her from doing anything else. Etcetera, I think, though another book I've been reading explains that each member of my class has spun maybe one step to the side since we've written our stories and mailed them.

Listen, it says, because you live north of the equator, you slip eastward through each moment you move. On your street it's seven hundred miles an hour that the world is spinning, and, uncorrected, you could slide to your town's river and splash, Icarus of the physics book. I understand. When I walk my mile to school I correct for the quarter inch of slide, allowing for slippage so I don't miss where I'm walking again and again like a child's first day of baseball, a father finding a fat, red, plastic bat, saying, "Here now, try this," and guiding his pitch to where he anticipates the arc, believing he knows the strange physics of children.

Such spinning that flings us sideways. I discover, among my class, a list of our early dead, someone whose wife has died, someone with a daughter killed, and I say goodbye to all of the clipped-from-my-yearbook absent as if they might have moved south, choosing another hemisphere so that they might twist backwards, slide the other way until we might see each other again, a sort of heaven rounding the planet from the opposite side.

Inertia

Each night the senior's dream of sex and blood,
Waking to the groin buzz at the temples
While high school deflated and I believed
Something, for once, might change. And that winter,
On my life's coldest morning, Gus Brickner,
The Human Polar Bear, lowered himself
Into the Monogahela River.
He swam and smiled. He stammered bare-chested
And dripping beside a thermometer
That claimed eighteen below. The weatherman
Shivered and joked until I turned him off
And walked to the school bus stop, hearing snow
Squeak like mice under my Converse All-Stars.
The bus driver motioned me to hurry,
But I kept listening. He waved and honked,
And after I slowed, he hissed the door shut
And drove. Thinking how that school bus might slide
Off the highway and plunge through river ice,
I watched for faces at windows and saw
Nobody, remembered how the Ice Age
Had driven glaciers to right where I was
Standing; how they had receded without
Reaching the spot where, an hour south of me,
Gus Brickner was probably repeating
"Enough"; how you could verify their length
By examining the sides of pits dug
In the earth like the craters for the start
Of missile silos in America
Or Russia. Or Cuba's photographed holes,
Unfilled just before that winter began.

Entropy

Because my mother has died, because I visit
To comfort my father, who refuses to move
One thing she owned, I see how Christmas stalled at gifts
Opened but unpacked, how her medicine's arranged
By frequency: Crystodigin, Diaranese,
Almodet (once daily); Cytomel (three times per day).
Duties with the weak heart. Percoset (as needed,
For severe pain, no refills), and I wonder at
The gap between the heart's demands. Then Nitrostat
(As needed, for chest pain), those pills the films' foolish
Grope toward as they tumble one room from relief,
This urgency of labels leveled to a kind
Of democracy, a haze of help from which nothing
Can emerge. Although I've learned my own medicine
From the tablets I take, twice daily; the capsules
I swallow, as needed; and the vapor I breathe
In the lapsed-lung darkness, lying back like Proust, whose
Life I've learned for my job, whose asthma bedded him
For years. He didn't take Theolair, Optimine,
Ventolin; insisted, finally, a huge black
Woman was chasing him. So she caught him. So now
My father strains to speak, tries, "Well, did you sleep good?"
To unmuzzle the morning, and I answer him,
"Good enough," as if truth might trigger prescriptions,
As if accidentally we might talk, as needed,
Swallowing to save our faulty selves, carefully
Speaking from the confluence of our altered blood.

Brouwer's Theorem

This snow is nothing
but an hour's cover.
Where I walk, the grass
returns, and these prints
that don't refill point
nowhere dangerous
unless I should last
a thousand miles north,

as far as I've been:
Beaupre, St. Anne's shrine
stacked up with crutches.
I trudged by braces
while it snowed in May.
I took color slides
and considered each
premonition pain
in my doubter's limbs,
how nothing there could
repair any part
of me, so far north
that week I retraced
the minus steps, ones
that lead right up to
the vanishing point,
something else we learn,
paying attention
to the snow lecture,
perspective lesson.

Perpetual Motion

Once upon a time, in the public schools,
There were Sputnik children, closed in classrooms
Until someone learned to launch satellites
That would orbit forever. We were trapped
Between science and math, waiting, waiting
For Rumplestiltskin to spin our homework
Into gold. He never arrived, of course,
But this winter my Chicken Little son
Is saying he fears the fall of space junk,
That the Russians could kill him as he sleeps
Dreaming himself into old age photos.
Tithonus, I think, one more fairy tale,
Although I tell him we're safe, ignorant
And lying as if I expect Villard's angel
To turn, to keep turning, to swivel
Its way toward eternity like myth.

How ludicrous the theories, and how we
Hypothesize again, guessing Bobby,
Billy, Jack, and Dave as if we were rich
With chances, as if machinery were
As simple as common names. That promise
Wheel was whirled by hammers, surrogates for
Water, and Villard moved nothing at all.
There were rockets on the television news
That tumbled and exploded and locked us
Tighter to physics and calculus, and
Now I'm starting one more wheel, expecting
A miracle even though the demon
Of foolishness has caught me by the shirt
To show me how easily things are jammed:
The dream of building. The dream of these words
We use, believing they sound like something
That goes on as perfectly as singing
In your head the records you love, sounding
Exactly like Ivory Joe Hunter,
Like Jessie Belvin, like Johnny Ace, names
From another kind of children's story.
I have blueprints on my desk; I'm writing
To scale and I'm failing to form all sides
At once as if the blind spots of migraine
Pinwheel through my translation. And I think
There is failure in this paper and ink,
The letters level as always, precise
As store displays, nothing for sale or use
Though we believe them voices, time lines drawn
From page to page to page like hammer wheels,
Satellites, the extrapolation dreams.

The Donora Geomancy

In 1948, nineteen people died in Donora, Pennsylvania,
during a weekend of heavy smog.

By reading the scattered patterns of seeds or sand,
By inspecting leaves or twigs, by tossing small things
In numbers and guessing, we might foresee
The first day of suffocation, the coughing
Furious throughout the thick, postwar inversion.

No one, then, read seriously a splash of stones.
No one murmured and looked up, terrified to moans
By the crossed and parallel handful. No one
Sang the prophecy of bone, Donora's deaths
At the end of the history of ruined lungs.

Now we regather the ashes to carry them
Like icons, renege the lead of the waste future.
Now we pursue the smogged, discredited past,
The quiet struggle of zinc workers who perform
The gasp chorus before smother interrupts.

Donora locked in power's smoke-filled room, hidden
In closets and under beds; Donora pulling
The sick to adrenalin's miracle,
Pushing the old to the great divining
Of flowers scattered over a drop of coffins.

On the hillsides, the last, late cabbages in soot;
On the hillsides, sheep gone black where anyone
Could carry remnants from the wire works
In his fist, shake them loose upon the ground
Which bears no grass, and begin to study.

Five days of pollution's narrowed throat. Five days
In the dry mist which rehearses the wheeze and pause
On the four-step staircase, the afternoons
Of the darkness funerals where mourners
Pay attention to the coughed prayers of neighbors.

And not prayer, but rain which scoured back shadows
Into the day. Not prayer, but the zinc works shutdown.
And so short a closure, so short the rain, so few
Moved away in the following months, the world
Returned to its own assurances:

Belief in beads, belief in tumbled ash and bone,
Faith of the hundreds who recovered, the thousands
Who suffered unrecorded, who worked again,
Comforted by how the near-dead revived, how grief
Is not compulsory in the age of science.

The Great Chain of Being

"Three generations of imbeciles are enough."
Oliver Wendell Homes, 1927

Too Little Air

There, on her carpet, we sat
Our year-old sons, and my cousin
Watched me count the handicaps
In her first-born until I froze
Like four legs in the headlights.
An accident, the doctor had
Told her, too little air, citing
The brief thesaurus of cause.
I nodded like someone saving
His job in an office of lies.
Her son crawled like he'd lighted
On the huge, invisible web
Of God. "My sister's boy has
A problem, too," she murmured.
"Both of us are moving closer
To cities so this never
Happens again." Too little air
In Pennsylvania, in Georgia.
Too little air in the room
Where we stared from one boy to
The other, so quiet, so long,
We might have been practicing
Conservation, as if that room
Had been sealed by landslide, and
We were finding the essential,
Slow rhythms of survival.

Vulcan and the Fire King

Planet Vulcan had to be there, hidden between
Mercury and the sun. What else, according to
Newton, could vary an orbit? What better name
For a planet so close to molten, in theory,

A hideout where Satan might be perfecting hell?
But when Vulcan stayed unspotted, the mystique of
Congruence stuck science to the keyhole until,
Soon enough, the impetus of impatience brought
The first sighting, the second, astronomers claiming
Discovery. There, they said, pointing the lens. There.

And there, the nineteenth century, fireproof women
And men headed playbills by surviving tortures,
Taking advantage of expectation's effect
On the eyes, one way we tend the infrastructure
Of error, relying, like Christians, upon
The necessity of the unobserved, as awed
As the audience for Chabert the Fire King, who
Climbed into his personal wood stove with raw steaks
And emerged, later, with a meal, well-done, sitting
To eat after visiting Vulcan's test kitchen.

Soon enough, a royal family of magicians
Could enter fire, reappear unscathed, diluting
The Bible with the commonplace of illusion.
Soon enough, the frequent tracts on explanation,
Scientists clamoring their revisionist clues
Until, finally, the appearance of the cage
Of fire, this wood stove open in front to appease
The jaded. There, they said, there he is, believing
Again, the Fire King standing in towering flames
Like the personification of a planet.

The Little Moron

In health class, eighth grade, we learned
The descending categories
Of the Stanford-Binet.
You couldn't do worse, if you
Made a mark, than idiot.
We knew one who loved lime soda
And laughed at the end of a leash
In his back yard. We saw imbeciles
Bused in and out of half-days

In the resource room, and we told,
In the halls, little moron jokes:

The little moron was playing
With matches and burned the house down.
"Your daddy's going to kill you
When he gets home," his mother said,
But the little moron laughed and laughed
Because he knew his daddy
Was asleep on the couch.

We laughed and laughed at everything
The little moron did. Why would
He take his ruler to bed? we asked.
He wanted to see how long he slept;
And he wanted, joke by joke,
To bring the dead metaphors
To life -- time, butter, and fire
Flying out his busy window.

"That will do," our teachers said.
"Three generations of imbeciles
Are enough," the Chief Justice said,
In 1927, supporting
The Eugenics Record Office,
Which wanted to sterilize everyone
Deemed unfit. Harry Laughlin,
Superintendent, hoped to eliminate,
In two generations, the submerged tenth
Of our population. He meant the blind,
The deaf, the orphans and the homeless;
He meant the poor and the stupid,
And the Supreme Court backed him up,
Finding a "clear and present danger"
In the family tree of the Bucks --
Who were illegitimate and poor;
Who were Emma, Carrie, and Vivian
Who made enough of these morons,
Declared deficient at seven months
After this expert testimony:

"There is a look about the baby
That is not quite normal, but
What it is I can't quite tell."

None of the Bucks, it turned out,
Was a moron like the one who took
His ladder to church for High Mass,
But Carrie's sister was sterilized,
Too, for good measure, and here is
The rest of the little moron's story:
He climbed and sat on top
Of his stepladder. He looked down
On the congregation, who were all
Looking down together. And looking
Down from the stepladder of research,
I can repeat the rosary
Of heredity, say *Fragile X,*
The syndrome which chains my cousins,
Their three imbecile boys, one
Generation enough, in this case,
For a chromosome passed down
Like a family job. That I'm
My mother's exception, in theory;
That my sister, who carries,
In theory, has no children.
That Vivian Buck managed
The honor roll in grade school
The year before she died. That chance
Blows the finest glass from this
Illusionist furnace, my gifted sons
Taking, like their father, those
Skip-a-grade intelligence tests.

The Verisimilitude of Purpose

Angels descend with lightning. The great fire
Of autumn signifies the bright palm prints
Of God. In Syria, five hundred years
After Christ, the infinite gradations
Of God's love were found in the natural

148

Light of all things by Dionysius
The Areopagite. The harmony
Of dusk and dawn. The iridescence of
The chosen. Even the angels absorbed
More or less of God's light, according to
Their nature, and they formed a chain of choirs
Graded toward glory. Who would believe in
The clumps and clusters of chance? And who would
Dare witness for the flaws of the learned?

In the Great Chain of Being, angels move
Above us, brutes below. Edward Tyson,
Comparative anatomist, believed
He verified the church's sleight-of-hand.
He studied a chimpanzee, expecting
The link which hooked to man's. One thing it liked,
Happily, was wearing clothes, a good sign
For the brute next door. And the first night out
At the bar, it drank itself to all fours,
Then altogether down, comfortable
With vice. Drinking is fine, Tyson explained,
But this damned knuckle-walking has to stop
Before you can model for the Great Chain
Encyclopedia: Practice . . . practice . . .
Tyson needed that chimp to walk upright,
Something snug between the large apes and us
For the arpeggio of the Great Chain.
But in one of Tyson's old plates, the chimp
Uses a walking stick; in another,
It ambles away, holding a rope stretched
Overhead like a commuter's hand rail.
And as for the pants? In hours, they reeked, were
Changed, then stunk again, refusing to chord.

Those chimps were exotic as Africans,
Who were one step above them, several steps
Below the British in the writings of
Charles White, biologist, who needed,
A century later, the alcohol
Of theory to enter the fire of doubt.

The Great Chain of the Upright, he bellowed,
The eighteenth century ended, the jaws
And foreheads of the apes translating as
"Africans." The American Savage
Was next, the Oriental its neighbor.
And White worked his way, by facial features,
To Europe, and, by extrapolation,
To the Greek ideal in antiquity.

Here was an apparition of theories,
The verisimilitude of purpose.
Praise orangutans, he published, because
They submit to bloodletting. Praise them twice
Because they take the African as slave.
Damn the sweat (not enough) and smell (too much)
Which binds Africans to the brutes. And as
For intelligence? In the golden age
Of assigned place, the white man bound to God,
Form followed function. And once, I had to
Recite the heroic couplets of Pope,
Passages chosen from "Essay on Man."
The Great Chain of Being jangled and clanked
Until the bored superior beings
"Show'd a Newton as we show an ape,"
Another thin theory taken to heart,
Immanuel Kant, in the Charles White years,
Looking to Jupiter, the planet of
Sufficient size to support God's higher
Beings, links between us and the angels.

The Gifted Test

The year I was asked to skip a grade,
The tester asked for the quick recall
Of body parts, current events, and
Trivia. For science, I mentioned
Ptolemy, the sun as God's spotlight;
I sequenced Copernicus, the church,
And Galileo. He smiled and read
Me puzzles like the one about Bill

Meeting his mother-in-law's only
Daughter's husband's son. What relation,
He questioned, is this person to Bill?
His son, I blurted, not bothering
With the proffered pencil, and I thought
He'd be astonished because I could
Calculate, in seconds, the equal
Number of quarters, dimes, and nickels
To get nine dollars and sixty cents.
I knew how many 9s I had to pass
Counting from 1 to 100,
And how to slosh water back and forth
From five quarts to three to finish
With exactly four. I thought the expert
Loved my top-scale score, would show me off
To every teacher in the district,
But my parents voted *no* and *no*
Before he spoke. That winter I built,
After a snowstorm, a model of
The solar system, according to
Johann Kepler, in our yard, rolling
And shaping the huge ball of Jupiter,
The extraordinary mound of the sun.
I worked the planets to scale, measured
Circumference and the distance from sphere
To sphere. I needed the neighbor's yard
For Pluto, and when the frost planets
Seemed plain, I gave them their moons to scale,
Snow berries and packed pebbles of ice.
At the end of the street I snowballed
Another star. I stood a hundred
Million miles from it, thought of my house,
And readied myself for ignition
Because surely, in all that snow, some
Life had formed and evolved to greet me.

House Wrens

My cousin was telling me about progress, care, and love. Her husband
was tossing a ball to our ten year-olds, casually and carefully by turns. A

step closer, a step back, handicapping the distance. My son, later, listed
all of the unlucky signs of coordination and speech, the long face and
big, floppy ears of the donkey. And later still, this year, my son in college,
hers on clean-up crew, and two other cursed boys from her sister,
heredity taking three branches where the gypsy moth of chance laid its
eggs, we bunch at our reunion where that trio flaps frantic with motion.
One of them knows the name of every bird at the feeder by the pavil-
ion. I'm told to say "What's that?" each time one settles, and he shouts,
"House wren," waves his hands, bites them, screams "House wren" for
the next and the next, laughs and laughs at my ignorance. And whether
it's the same bird, three different ones from the same species, or he's
bluffing like a parrot, I ask again, looking to where my own sons are
throwing horseshoes for the first time, already bored with *ringer, leaner,*
the simple language of play.

Stitches

Turning into teens, we bunched in those last
Vacant lots beside the tracks where no one

Would build. Beneath our feet, the cackling of
Eggshell glass, the rasp of cinders, static

Through the retelling of improbable
Erotic stories, the tentative beer

And Camels keeping us perched on the lines
Scratched in the dirt where Holt and Benko fought,

One of them snapping enough right hands to
The face to etch humiliation.

Benko crawled. He bleated until a tail
Grew behind him, until his lips disappeared

And all we saw were teeth just before he sprang
Snarling with a brick, opening forty

Stitches worth of gouge through Holt's crew-cut scalp.
And that exam-nervous night, none of us

Knew what we recollected while Holt told
His parents about plunging from a tree.

And then we wished for wounds, the thin sweat tracks
On our chests turning scarlet the next time

We practiced the tumbling agony of
The stunt man down each return-home hillside,

Hearing the highway diesels drive by tough
As armies, clutching ourselves when we rose

Where prefab houses were exploding from
Shell craters, and there, in variations

We could not see, our features would crawl up
Inside us like shy, unwanted birthmarks.

What the Lecturer Showed Us

Some mornings the chimpanzees skip breakfast,
Hike as one to where the Aspilia grows.
They gibber reluctance, chatter complaints
Of bitter and vile, but all of them gulp
Its leaves, clean a branch like children frightened
By the household god of famine-to-come.

The purgatives of the rain forest, home
Remedy for parasites, for fungi --
And we may smile, following them on film
Carried here by science -- but now, we learn,
The oil of the Aspilia destroys
The malignant cells of certain tumors.

Thus, we're instructed by the pharmacy
Of the primates, watch the sick chimp who drags

Herself to the foul bush of Vernonia
To chew its leaves, swallow the juice. We cheer
Her next day recovery, how she grooms
Herself again and forages for food.
And, of course, in the natural selection
Of medicinal plants, the ignorant
And stupid will swallow poisonous leaves,
End their faulty genes with an incorrect
Prescription. Pay attention, survivors
Lecture, to pattern, color, texture, scent.

Eat these stems during the rainy season.
Take two of these petals for climate change.
And here are the aids for fertility,
Their counterparts for prevention. And there
Are the howling monkeys who can diet
For daughters or sons, who eat acidic

Or alkaline to shift conception odds
For the x or the y of sperm. Watch those
Howlers who feel betrayed, perhaps, or trapped.
They grind the leaves for induced abortion,
Take care of themselves without consulting
Doctors, lawyers, politicians, or priests.

The Polygamy of Doubt

In the polygamy of doubt, we see the overhead wires
Of the rope trick, the man who threads it upward.
Some snake charmers, cautious, sew shut their cobras' mouths
And perform hourly, racing starvation and the next
Careful stitching. And certainly, though Tyson's chimp
Never got drunk again, some animals lack discipline,
The elephants who go back to beer, chug twenty at a time
To forget, some theorize, the end of the open range.

Someone else claims the dinosaurs forgot everything
But the drugs of flowering plants in the centuries
They first flourished. Those lizards gorged and got high;
They overdosed and died in an apocalypse of the giants.

We've laughed and laughed at their idiot ways, more
Foolishness in the great chain of brutes who rattle
The links of their life spans -- the sestina of dog years,
The sonnet of the hamster, the haiku of the may fly.

And we believe so much in the epic of our lives,
The photographs, the slides, and the long pauses
For our stories which enlarge the past until our memories
Are edited to accept the anthropic principle, how
Everything has led to us, the fingernail filings,
In one image, of the king's long arm of time,
Entering one more theory as if we were the magicians
Who amaze by slipping *into* impossible restraints.

X

My uncle keeps a chart of ancestors,
My mother's great, great grandfather series,
Their occupations parenthetical
Beneath their life-spanned names. Tailor, tailor,
Tailor, it says, fading like an echo
Through the nineteenth century and stopping,
1782, in Germany,
Five generations fixed in one village
Before the coming to America.

The great chain of a construct. All but one
Of them died from lung disease; I use
An inhaler for cats, pine trees, the dust
From these redundant flow charts, checking for
Myself in my mother, my sons in me,
Until the white linen of reunion
Settles us, and my cousins, the mothers
Of imbeciles, watch their husbands cut ham,
Butter corn, prevent their sons from choking.

When Einstein accounted for the shifts in
Mercury's orbit, the Vulcan sightings
Ceased. Someone works, now, to identify
The monkey gene. And on a million hats,

This year, the X of a dead man who worked
To break one version of the static chain
Of being. And in some illustrations,
The X of the early cross worshipped by
All my cousins who take their sons to church.

On documents throughout the world, the X
Of the marks made by the illiterate,
Repeated and repeated, mimicking
The signature. And in the protective
Mimicry of nature, the viceroy looks,
Now, to most birds, like the monarch, the one
Butterfly they've learned not to eat because
It gorges, as a caterpillar, on
Poisonous plants. And even its name is

Mimicry, one more step in the art of
Disappearance we practice, vanishing
From the sight of angels who swoop down to
Comfort us. They see the near six billion
So similar we might all be noxious
Gathered here at the X which marks the spot
Where we've driven to celebrate births and
Anniversaries. And finally we
Assemble in one huge, rented room to

Face the camera of each parent. The light
Is weak and varied near the north window.
The children are sullen or self-conscious
Or bored with the afternoon's past. "Ok,"
I say, "ok," finding the three imbeciles
Who are gripped on the shoulders, two-handed,
By grandmother, mother, and carrier
Sister, each of those wild boys smiling
And still, momentarily, for my flash.

Forecasting the Dragon

When Huang Ti, the emperor, sent Hsi and Ho,
The imperial astronomers, to explore;
When they shipped out for every place east of China,
The lands of Fu Sang, to see if the heavens changed;
They sailed to America, west coast, arrived so
Long ago their voyage seems historical hoax.

When they tired of Guatemala, of Mexico,
Four thousand years before Commander Columbus;
When they made it back to China, they reported
To their boss, who listened and nodded and returned
Them to their science, to forecasting the dragon,
The one who crossed behind the sky to eat the sun.

When the solemn gongs still worked. When a multitude
Of clamor could retract eternal night if throngs
Gathered soon enough to drum fear in the serpent
And the sun's first missing mouthful were broadcast, what
Hsi and Ho were hired to know, dating the dragon,
Predicting its hunger for holy Huang Ti.

And when Hsi and Ho failed, the oriental sun
Bitten by surprise, the beaters not alerted.
When, bored by the familiar Chinese sky, they were
Drunk and delinquent, the silly world saved, this time,
By the delicate appetite of the dragon,
The two were executed by their lucky lord.

Or so one history says, although here, in others,
Are the Hindu missionaries in the New World,
Six hundred B.C., and Brendan, the Irish priest,
Five-fifty A.D., and then all of those Norsemen
Who came and went, sighting after native sighting
Of the strange-skinned seamen, the oddly-featured gods.
So many disembarkings of swords and armor,
Bibles and beards. So many indecipherable
Creatures, they turned as common as the green and blue,

The huge heads and slender bodies from the saucers
I read about on Sunday mornings, stopping, once,
At the true-life adventure of Joe Simonson,

To whom spacemen had given a pancake. I stared
At his photograph. He had the flapjack as proof,
Holding it up to the lens, and I was eating
Cereal, the breakfast of aliens, raising
My bowl as if posture and a double portion
Could transform my body into a rainbowed hulk.

Mary King, in England, had met Master Jesus,
Who had flown here from placid Venus to hand her
The Twelve Blessings of extraterrestrial love.
Her son, she claimed, was sacred, and anyone can
Guess the counterclaims, the scoffing, the tabloids' joy
Until the Mercurians flamed down in Belgium.

But when my neighbor, just now, tells me about lights
Where they could not be; when she describes colors in
The night woods, babble turned to language by her skin,
I say nothing of Pancake Joe, Jesus in space;
Nothing of Balboa, Magellan, how oceans
And continents were titled by selective claims,

Diaries turned to scriptures. These ships touch and flee
As if Earth's surface were shore. In each galaxy
Are Vespucci Papers from a thousand planets,
True histories of expeditions, the wonder
Of contact, the loss of faith, how the universe
Has been labeled, bit by bit, in a million tongues.

The Hunza Dream

The Hunza, from northwest Kashmir, are the only group
of people known to be free of cancer.

1

After this coal town lost its jobs,
After anthracite packed and fled,
The entrepreneurs arrived, wrote
Hydroponics on their government grant
For gardeners and glass, low-interest
Revitalization loans. Now hundreds
Of greenhouses lie on the leveled slag,
Tomatoes going green to pink, half
A million madly swelling out of water
Inside this paradise for vandals.

2

The last coal has wound its way eastward,
Lost itself to barge and train. A mile
From the greenhouses a culm-bank rises
Higher than any hill in the county,
Sits sparse of growth like the cancer-scalp
Come home from treatment for the hot spots
In the body when they flare like mine fire,
Rumors of bankruptcy, default on loans.
And this evening I watched those houses
From my steel-blue car, parked by myself
Like a lure for entrapment waiting for
Lights, the lonely, or the Quasimodo
Look of the law. And when the darkness clung
To the stalks, when none of those choices
Came, I backed, turned, and crept to the highway
As if I'd thrown a body from my trunk.

3

How we rock-a-bye our children
Through inevitable daymares,

My daughter blood-tested last week
And winning her lottery with
The mono ticket, seven days
Asleep instead of clinic drives.
And surely she understands that
Cells default, a boy she's danced with
Dying tonight a year after
Sitting for that needle. She's heard
His odds, at least, quoted, because
He hadn't mishandled canning,
Plutonium, or sex. She's seen
Eulogy write itself despite
Diet, safeguards, desire's control.
And after the doctors removed
His bone marrow, after they cleaned
And changed it to something he might
Live with, they put it back, and he
Brightened, then bloomed, then turned to husk.

4
Always, in the collective wish, there are parents
Reading the stories of the laying on of hands.
In this house, in those rooms, in that office their lips
Are moving to the rhythm of the faith-spun words
As if reading like children might ease the entrance
Of the Hunza dream. In the gospel of remissions
Is the prophecy of promise. In the gospel of cures
Is the hearsay miracle of the absent apostle.

Handing the Self Back

Maybe I can anticipate the sense
My son will make of me, writing
Thirty years from now
One of those poems about his father,
How he wished me dead or understood
Nothing because I never spoke.
The copyright on my moods
Will be hidden in his house,
Tucked back in his closet,
Rustling in the night to disturb
His sleep. He will wake angry
And unable to explain himself.

"This grease spot," my father said,
Pointing, "was a little boy
Who got too close," and I believed
Everything he said until
I could not listen, but I never
Saw poetry when I watched him
Haul bread from those ovens, and then
I was lost in a brockwork hate,
My language salvaged from the streets
That titled toward the mills.

No son understands how the ears go bad;
Already I cannot hear my own
When he stalks across the room,
A dark, brushstroked question.
So I concentrate each day
On not hitting him
With another simile,
"You're like a . . ." stuck
in my throat while I wrap myself
in the smoke-smell of paper logs
because I warm the house with trash.

It is always after the rain we walk,
Choosing a strange route
Until we have to go miles for change,
So in his poem we may be walking,
The last minute before turning back,
And he will use a rocket image,
The nosing over into gravity
Like code-chattering pilots.

And he will recall something
Like the rainbow grease spots
Or oil slicks, the sidewalk sad
With them as some of the windows
We pass, nothing we notice, open.
I will shrink through his stanzas;
I will shrivel into a raisin
In his memory or hang on, figurehead,
On a porch in Florida, robbing
His middle-age, and he will shame
Himself to approach the truth
From what he guesses is the front.

Calculating Pi

Pi has been calculated to 480 million decimal points — Newsweek

Printed out, this means six hundred miles of digits,
A paper carpet from Pittsburgh to Chicago
For high tech absurdists who might be tallying
The sheep they've imagined before sleep, the fat flock
They've columned and counted like the cartoon restless.

Who might be lapsing into the dreams the awake
Have: numbering loss, summing the hours, repeating
The simplest algorithms for despair. Who might
Be foolproofing the warhead, eliminating
Error, so deep in the silos the soldiers know

Their computers are exact, whether they're sending
The missiles to Moscow or its suburbs. Pi checks
For typos, dust specks, and cosmic rays. Pi's perfect.
Pi's a sitter's lullaby. Hush, it sings, don't cry,
Crooning soft verse to soft verse to infinity.

The REM Sleep of Birds

For years, no one was watching, when, in sleep,
The stories some suffered by night spun long
With plots that vanished. The REM-sleep novels
Erased themselves, turned to the wolf-child tales
Of the difference-wishful. Though there's good cause,
We've learned lately, to find yourself early
In those nightmares (the sooner, the smarter).
It's good to have narrative, metaphor,
Because the overdressed dream is a sign
Of the adult lurching from the mists of
Nursing and crying, awake in the crib
With no language to use on the woman
Who arrives to hover, float overhead
In her own feathered fear. Listen — now we
Know the rapid eye movement sleep of birds
Is more than flutter, that imagery slides
Through the ruffled darkness among the leaves
Where swallows dream of falling; starlings dream
Electrocution on the power line;
And sparrows dream of a world of windows,
Glass labyrinths, the insistence of flight.

Why We Care about Quarks

Because something deflected the fired electrons.
Because emptiness, suddenly, seemed crowded, and
The invisible, three bits of it, needed a name
After *aces* was rejected, that opener called
Before a fourth dot could fill the proton's hand.

Because some things can't be named by committee,
Approved, like *ampere*, like *moron*, by a show of hands.
Because one physicist had read *Finnegan's Wake*
And remembered "Three quarks for Muster Mark,"
German for cottage cheese or forced-rhyme Joycese.

Because an invisible zoo can be named by whim.
Because each quark could be christened like a pet:
Up, then *down*, then *strange*. Because *charm* was found.
Because *beauty*, the fifth, appeared on the doorstep,
And theoretical *truth* belongs above it.

Because there may be more, anything possible
Where the eye can't enter. Because symmetry
Builds models, and the octagon's fresh flavors
Will need to be named: *paradise*, for instance.
Eternity. As if the inferred, invisible

Structure were proof enough for the alleluias
Of hope. Because someone believes in the force
Of color, the power of purple or infrared
To bind as many as eighteen quarks, building
A tower or ladder or beanstalk which will

Surely lift us to the sky-blue ceiling, our children
Gathering to steady us from below as we feel
For the trapdoor seams, rap and listen for the hollow
Sound of entry, reciting immortality names
Like delirious disciples of ascension.

The Universal Language of Waiting

Ludwig Zamenhof, in the late nineteenth century, constructed Esperanto,
a language he hoped would become internationally used to diminish warfare.

My grandmother waited for her husband in German,
For the coming of Christ in Latin. Her neighbors sang
Or screamed in Slovak and Polish, Croatian and Czech,
Believing so much in the rhythms of love they banked
Their hearts like the furnaces in the long-struck mills.

Some of those women swept me close with their brooms to growl
The ground rules of sidewalks in gutturals that promised
To use one end or the other on my thoughtless face,
Their dogs snarling the same sentences of woe until
The street turned into the squalling radio of fear.

Some people suddenly speak a language not their own.
Some people start to write what they recall in spellings
That bond in the quick Spanish of the first Mexican
Family on Prospect Street listening to speech so strange
They thought everybody in Etna emigrated
From a village bound by the rope of related tongues.

A director, once, made a film in Esperanto,
Transforming dialogue to mystery, believing
Each exchange became as eerie as the incubus
Who stole the souls of sleeping women while he slathered
Each scene with subtitles or dubbed over flapping mouths.

That film waits for Esperanto's rise, the world joined hands
Around the campfire of common language. My grandmother
Told me, in English, about the eighty-pound ice heart
Omaha carved to lure Sonja Henie back to town,
How it's shrunk to sixty pounds, still warehoused, speaking to

The dead in the universal language of waiting.
Like Ludwig Zamenhof, who believed he could form peace
With the Yugoslavia of good intentions;

Like all those diplomats who listen on headphones
To simultaneous translations, each of their nods
Staggered by the varying degrees of rephrasing.

The Air of Delicate Pastry

Francis Battalia, years ago, ate stones
By the spoonful, chased them with beer and shook
The sack of his stomach for evidence.

Soon, stone eaters flourished. The thinnest drank
Water to flush their gravel, fueled one cult
Of reduced calories, early converts

To the slow furnace of zoologists
Who extend the lives of test mice, these days,
By diminishing their charted dinners.

In our country of sad diets, we choose
The stones of low sugar, low sodium,
The rocks of low fat and cholesterol.

We suck and roll them back our tongues to gulp
Doses for the fears which keep us cautious.
Which bite brings the AIDS of the arteries

Or the stiff botulism of the heart?
Though he made them, my father wouldn't eat
The fat ladylocks and thick whoopie pies,

Refusing their sweet, white sculptures of creme.
Lard and sugar, he told me. A little
Water. Fool's food, he said, like the corn starch

Of bargain pies, the refined sweeteners
Of icing he tasted, judged, and spit out
While he slathered it for millworkers,

Baking from midnight till morning, stopping
With doughnuts turning gold in the deep-fat
Fryer. He ate wheat bread, the rich custard

Of eclairs. He explained fiber and eggs
And the legitimate sugars of fruit.
And he praised the natural holes in bread,

None of them like the homogenized air
Of Wonder loaves, their dough a miracle
Of emulsifiers, whipped and balanced

Like flavored scoops of soft ice cream, perfect
Squares of processed cheese. And then he described
The air of delicate pastry, how it

Lightens the richness of butter, how he
Folded and sheeted, folded and sheeted
Until that sweet dough spread so fine and light

It released the breeze of desire, the breath
Of gratitude, what works to support us,
The air from which we never grow estranged.

Enlisting

Every list came to school:
milk, dimes, savings bonds.
On the teacher's desk
sat the bathroom list,
the fountain list.
They'd squeal on you.
They'd tell Miss Hartung
you were smoking or carving
filth on a wall.
There was a list in the air
that beat up sissies,
that circled Harold Martin
and signed him up
for a second tour
while the list for teams
chased us across a field,
yelled from the bleachers,
stood by the sidelines
in a gang. We shrunk
inside our uniforms,
hit and curled by tackles,
air nowhere near our lungs.
Not then. And not while
those lists were posted,
the ones that flew us
to Asia, the third
of seven continents
on a list we copied
from Harold Martin,
who stopped reporting us
after he read our list
all over his unprotected,
third-world body.

Class A, Salem, The Rookie League

We were drinking for free, bumming beers
From the past-their-prime by claiming
Ourselves Pittsburgh prospects, fireballers
Who'd broken in, last summer, in Salem.
We'd gotten a look in Columbus,
Three innings each in a courtesy game.
"Candelaria," we said, taking
Refills. "What a party he threw
When the Pirates called him up that night."

We settled for Iron City, draft mugs.
It was semester break, sophomore year.
In three weeks, pitchers like us were due
In Bradenton, Florida, to prove
Ourselves for Double or Triple A,
And we wouldn't come back to this bar
At Easter unless the two of us
Were released, disabled, or home
For a sudden death in the family.

We said my mother was sick, my friend
Had a tender arm. We said we'd leave
Tickets for this tavern if either
Of us made Three Rivers, and drank four nights,
Underage, with men who supported us
Like fathers. They wanted names, whom

To expect from Salem in three years,
The vets we'd met on their falls to sandlots,
Factories, or bars like Emerico's,
Where they'd name, in turn, Al Oliver,
Dock Ellis, or the Steve Blass Syndrome,
Cite the strange, sad case of his lost control.

We were twenty miles from our old school,
Two districts from any fans we knew,
But there, one midnight, sat Mrs. Cook,

Giving us her speech-class, critical look.
She could have offered *slower, louder,*
Breath control. She could have recited
A roll call of our gradebook names, summoned
Us to the front of a fist-filled room
With the forensic demand for truth.

Glazed-green, the bar's surface suggested
Sea stories where the careless drown
In a tangle of cramps. We carried
A beer to her booth like homework;
One of the men who loved baseball
Slid in beside her. "From the Pirates,"
We said, trying to enunciate
Like athletes, setting our last story
Deep as we could in the farm system.

The Local Cemetery

I went by myself, late
In the summer, looking
At first, over my shoulder
Like some clumsy spy.
I walked to the brightest
Cut flowers and paid
Attention to last week's date,
The name of a woman
From my street. Her husband
Had come here yesterday.
He had looked, I supposed,
At his dates, 1920-199_,
Giving himself four years,
And I have been with my father
When he stood on the grass
And said, "You can always
Find me here." He gestured
And meant me to think
Of the nearby plot as mine;
I kept walking and found
Whole families, like ours,
Together for a hundred years,
Settled in from Europe
And never moving again,
Never thinking of moving,
And even now, my sister
Has moved back to Pittsburgh,
Two miles from my father,
And asks when I'm coming home,
Says she has purchased space
In the Garden of Dreams,
Which, so far, leaves me out,
Kicking the earth hundreds
Of miles away, picking up
The one stone I've seen in all
Of this grass and sailing it
Into the trees where it rattles
And falls into silence.

From THE ALMANAC FOR DESIRE
(2000)

The Dark Angels

To the sidewalk in front of my father's
Razed bakery I return. To the patch
Of burdock where the stacked ovens deep-browned
The crusts of a million loaves and rolls.
To the cinderblock cracked like the soot-pocked
Windows where I watched, in Etna, the dark
Angels escape the coal smoke as if they
Wanted to swoop back to chimneys. To shards
And splinters where I hated the sauerkraut
In the cramped, next-door kitchen, the boiled
Shank end of pork which clustered flies against
The latched screen door. To the steep, shale downslope
Where the walls of the bakery are landfill,
Where the first bulldozed soil coats wallboard
And lumber as if coal were refueling
Industry's return, covering the spot
Where I was careless, once, with Saturday's
Trash fire. Where it followed the easy weeds
To the brittle boards of the bakery.
Where the neighbor shook free the flies and sprayed
His hose and a set of obscenities
Keyed to my foolish name. Where my father
Thanked him and led me to the last eclair,
Settled me on the work room's folding chair
And said nothing except "think," and I thought
That neighbor was listening at the window
While I held chocolate and custard until
My father said, "You eat that," and I did.

The Holy Numbers

We listened, as always, to Pastor Dave,
learning the Bible's major numbers, one
through the nine sixty-nine of Methuselah,
who lived eight times longer than all of us
put together. We memorized the three
parts of the Trinity, the four Gospels.
We recited the Ten Commandments
and the names of the twelve disciples,
subtracting Judas the Betrayer
before we matched them to the eleven
of ourselves, the future fishers of men.
Pastor Dave told us sacrifice stories,
the number of ways to be crucified,
including upside down, but the five boys
wanted to know the number of minutes
Jesus lasted on the cross, the number
of stones it took to slaughter Stephen.
Pastor Dave made us recite the Nicene
and the Apostles Creed, listening for
lapses because we were the future
of a faith which could spout, in unison,
the sixty-six books of the Bible,
ending with Revelation and its lists
of sevens and twelves. And I wanted
to ask the number of men who'd taken
Mary Magdalene to bed, and how much
she charged. And not asking, I counted,
on my own, the years I had until
three score and ten, learned the date for Easter
in 2015, when I needed
to rise from the dead and be repaid
for the 10% I'd been taxed by God.
Because I didn't see myself among
the nine groups blessed by Beatitudes,
not the boys who were poor in spirit;
not the meek we taunted; not the six girls
who were pure in heart, their bodies numbered

by breasts and thighs when the boys picked partners,
choosing until one was unchosen,
becoming the Virgin Mary, shifting
in her chair as if she were already
counting the two major heart attacks
of Pastor Dave, the three weeks between them,
the forty-two years he lived, including
the twenty-seven days after he laid
his hands to our heads and declared us saved.

The Natural Method of Dog Training

"Torture, which was once a craft, has become a technology."
Dr. Timothy Shallice

1

My mother said "Accept no rides from strangers.
Don't even approach an unfamiliar car."
My father told me his search-party story,
The naked boy found, too late, tied to a tree.
The tongue was pulled from his throat; the lines still breathe:
"You never catch those drivers," my father said,
Yet I stood at the roadside, thumb extended,
And he swerved at me so suddenly I took
The guardrail with the step and leap of panic.

2

To teach, according to the slim manual
For *The Natural Method for Dog Training,*
You lay tacks on the furniture, covering
The forbidden places for sleep. You throw
Firecrackers from your moving car to keep
That dog off the road. You spray it with a hose.
You place rat traps among the roses where
Digging's not allowed. And when nothing works,
You starve the animal to show who's boss.
It will come begging, then, apologetic
And compliant. You will own a well-trained dog.

3

When the general came to our school,
When he lectured us at the assembly
About the A-bomb and the safety
Of America, he called radiation
"Cloudshine" to honor the sky's pink glow.
One teacher, when the science fair
Arrived, told us a girl in Utah,
The year before, brought the head and neck
Of a cow for her exhibit, those parts

Split open to show the tumors
Which had murdered her father's herd.
In another part of the country
A man hypothesized hormesis,
The therapy of low-level rads
To toughen us toward longer lives.
Pantywaist, sissy, mama's boy--
We were still using, to cure cowardice,
The old therapy of namecalling.
Pansy, fairy, faggot, queer--
The double-dare of the schoolyard
And boot camp made it easier
To gut than go home, to shoot than say NO.
Trial and error. School of hard knocks.
We cry or don't cry. We grin and bear it
Or we scream and run. No pain, no gain,
Like the man whose leg cracked last night
When he lifted the most weight of his life.
We put our fingers to the flame;
We lay them on the coils just after
The red fades. So our lives will be better,
So we can distinguish right from wrong
And be numbered among the saved.

4

Once upon a time, doctors pulled the foreskin
Over the tip of the penis, punched holes
And stitched it to prevent masturbation.
That will do for now, they said to parents.
He'll think twice or pay the penalty
Of pain for allowing sin's tumescence.
There were remedies, from the beginning,
For every carnal crime, including
The natural method of castration,
So effective, so long, it was used
On epileptics and the insane.
Weren't seizures just sexual release?
Didn't the original sin of sex
Propel the weak to mental illness?
"The most significant factor

In social reform in history"--
What one expert declared just as
The era of the electric chair
Began, just as civilization was
About to be rid of capital crimes.

5
In the history of aversion therapy,
In the celebrated cases when cures
Were claimed, the physicians always speak:
Like Alexander Morrison, the champion
Of camphor oil, his patients swallowing
Their way to sweating and vomiting,
Diarrhea, convulsions. "That does it,"
He said, publishing his lectures to acclaim,
How he followed the progress of nine men
Who practiced "the crime against nature."
The way they took their dose with the sight
Of naked men. The way two of them changed,
Or so they said, cured of one kind
Of insanity. The way the lust
Of seven was so severe they stayed
Aroused, near-death, by anything male.
Like John Wesley, who ministered
With the electric friction machine
To save the worst of his Methodist flock.
"The unparalleled remedy," he said,
Preaching the gospel of therapy
As if it were one more metered phrase
For a hymn, the one in progress while
He watched the hair rise on the lunatics
Of little faith, those who might be rescued
From hell by small bolts of holiness,
Something like the practices of Saint Rose,
Who wore a chastity belt for life,
Who threw away the key and daily
Whipped herself. Who ate poisons, then fasted
Near death. Who disfigured herself. Who wore
A hair shirt and a crown of thorns. Who dragged
With her a wooden cross, preceding

St. Marina, not outdone, who added,
To her belt, spikes and iron teeth.

6
In one test, snails were fed a food
They'd never tasted, given two hours
Before sickened by injection.
Always, after that, they refused
That dinner, even weeks later,
A long stretch for the memories
Of snails. And surely the patients
Who vomit recall, outstripping
The snails, memorizing like birds
Who retrace the migration paths
Or die; like deer who recollect
The proper winter trails or starve.
In California, in the late Sixties,
In the state hospitals at Vacaville
And Atascadero, patients were
Softened by Anectine, overdosed,
With or without a medical release:
Complete paralysis, breathing stopped
For three minutes, subject still conscious,
The better to be conditioned by
The suggestions of the doctors.
"An extremely negative experience,"
One witness said, yet those sex offenders,
Those criminally insane, were told,
When released, the do-it-yourself
Therapies of snapping rubber bands
Against their wrists, shoving fingers
Down their throats when unorthodox
Sex thoughts began. And, for tough cases,
The do-it-yourself of a shock machine
Made portable. "Useful in the playground"--
How the catalogue put it while I was
Busy with monkey bars and swings,
All that playground metal conducting
Improved behavior through my childish frame.
That did it, not the collective shock

Which worsened us, not the sad siren
Of civil defense, the tight tuck
In the stairwell, or the sprawl behind
The green dumpster when caught outside.
For improvement, you needed to be
Singled out, to cry where everyone
Could see you, every wail as visible
As a stain spreading from the crotch.

7

So late in December, so cold
across the full width of Ohio,
I was working up the self-pity
of "casualty," equating myself
with the sleepers on sidewalks.

So long between rides, I skipped
pre-scanning the driver to see
what he might charge, a policeman,
the car unmarked, or a man
in uniform aroused by boys.

I used classroom diction. I kept
eye contact with the highway,
the border five miles away. And when
we passed the welcome sign, not slowing,
I thought I was a sadist's dream.

In Pennsylvania, where I was
heading, a man had entered the homes
of women with a store-bought badge.
He let them live to be witnesses,
all six repeating boots and blue hat,

the dark-brown holster, none of them
remembering a face. "You know you're
illegal," he said, while I studied
chin and nose, a scar below the ear.
"If I choose," he said, "I'll make you pay."

Two days to the new year, that car
unheated to keep him up, I poured
the night sweats of the terminal.
He listed bus and train, the relative
safeties of ticketed rides.

Outside, ambiguous snow swirled up,
then cleared. He said he had pictures
of a boy flung into a landfill,
the work an overnight of rats
can do. He said "Look under the seat"

and I didn't. He said "End of the line,"
slowed, and the animals of evening
said nothing while I filled the door.
They might have been listening for
the sweet groans of dawn while he u-turned,

while he opened his window and drove
the soft shoulder like a mailman
to deliver a photograph
which brushed me, then fluttered between
his tire tracks, face down like choice.

8
Throughout high school, story after story
About radiation sickness, the short
And long term of it in Nevada
And Utah, testimonials from
Survivors about a smorgasbord
Of cancer and government denials.
And one story, finally, about
The benefits of uranium, how
It pulls diseases from the body,
Sending patients into played-out mines
For the cure of the abandoned cave.
And then a rush of precedents, including
The claims of Elisha Perkins,
Who held a patent on The Tractor,
Two rods which drew disease from the body

185

By the mix and alignment of alloys,
How they were held, lowered and raised
Like the palms of Christ or the surrogates
Who placed their healers' hands and prayed
At sunrise service, telling the tumors
To follow the sun. And there were
Testimonials, a neighbor's breast
Restored, an uncle's tumor shrunk.
And whether those old recoveries
Proved those rods responsible,
Whether cure lasted for hours or years,
George Washington, for one, believed,
Bringing his family to the early version
Of the uranium cure, though he was bled,
Just before death, by his doctors,
Submitting to basic extraction,
What could be verified, not
The possible pull of alloys, not
The wishful benefits of the unseen.

9

Coach said to drink no water
during practice. We'd cramp,
he said, and water guzzlers
were losers who would run
from battle. He'd witnessed
foxhole fear, the piss and moan
of cowardice. There was war
waiting for us in Asia,
and nobody on this team
would do less than good, he'd see
to that, fifteen laps, fast breaks,
a scrimmage, and the night
he switched us into darkness,
lit flares in four corners
of the gym. You keep that ball
moving, he said. You take it
to the hole and crash those boards,
firing his starter's pistol,
advancing while we screened

and rolled, moved without the ball,
more than ready, he said,
to invade any school
who thought "battle-tested"
was just a chalk-talk phrase.

10
After the expanded war stripped
our student deferments, we sold
self-pity in the flea market
of the dispossessed, borrowing
lake front for beer and girls we hoped
to seduce with new-world sorrow.
By summer we'd be refugees,
selected so low by lottery
we'd lug a small part of ourselves
to a bus and listen for rules.
Those girls would finish college or not,
but that day one of them coupled
so close, so much in a clearing,
we thought she'd pull a train of soldiers.
One of us walked our proposal
forward like a diplomat, that girl
so still I thought my friend had killed her.
I heard "all yours," numbers up to six,
my voice assigning my place in line.
Suddenly, each of the other girls smoked.
The sky became a two-way mirror.
As if heaven were behind it, I stared,
repeating what I'd bid on, turning
away, drinking and looking across
the water as if glare were important.
I could see better with my back turned,
remembering dogwood, the burgundy
of that blanket, the fraternity crest
centered under her passive thighs.
I erased dandelions with my shoes.
And when I heard Number Six walk away
I didn't flinch, so he could have left
or helped that girl, because when I turned,

finally, the empty space had reformed
among those sweet-scented, flowering trees.

11
A week later, a whore in Cleveland
asked me what I wanted for ten dollars,
whether I was scared or queer, hesitant
in Hough, where race riots were months away.
I was playing my last tournament
tennis for a church-related college.
The next morning I would lose my match
to the one black player in the conference,
and what was I accomplishing
with my doubles partner, the two
of us so white outside the blues bar
we festered like pimples shut up
by stupidity and cowardice.
I said there was nothing she could do
worth ten dollars, said it so measured
and clear to myself that my partner
agreed when I stepped off the curb,
skittering beside me the three blocks
back to where the races mixed, then,
more slowly, three more to where we slept.
"Edison Medicine," I said, quoting
the one person I'd met who'd been sent
to shock treatment. "Look here," he'd murmured,
so softly and so soon after
he'd picked me up, I thought he'd opened
his pants or his set of photographs
would feature nude boys, not Edison's
early film, the electrocution
of an elephant. Didn't I know
the first electric chair was built
at Menlo Park? Didn't I know
they tested dogs and horses and cows
before the first prisoner took minutes
to literally cook? Didn't I see
my body as meat? "You look in the back,"
he said, "and guess," and I swiveled,

saw milk cans, and said nothing at all
while he described the explosions
they'd make if we wrecked or tore through
the wrong Ohio pothole. I was
considering the crimes of elephants
and the ones I'd been lately committing.
"Has you thinking, doesn't it?" he said,
right about that, offering beer
with the early warning of attack,
making me think of opening my door
like a school bus driver each time
we reached a set of railroad tracks.
I didn't ask out. I didn't ask for
the next bottle from the six pack
between the worn seats, tough enough
to flee Youngstown, Ohio, with
the cargo of possible bombs.
Just before my school, the neighborhood
turned to bones. Forty minutes I'd worked
to ask no questions. In two more,
I knew the pedestrians I'd meet,
the likely rides if I decided
to leave again. Behind barbed wire
one night shift had parked a lot full.
Pretend you're driving to work, I said
to myself, imagining I could use
the machinery inside those walls,
identical sculptures lurching by
on black, rubber belts, all of us
busy with building the one thing.

12
Now I can buy a video filmed
From a dog's point-of-view, the camera,
Apparently, two feet from the ground,
The subjects those a dog should love:
A duck chase, car rides, a cattle roundup.
"A tape," the brochure claims, "your dog can watch
Over and over," twenty-five minutes
A long time for my dog to watch

Anything unless I train her,
Unless she knows to stay put, flattened
Against the car floor when we cross gravel,
What she hears at the kennel, at the vets.
The way my first son, not quite two,
Screamed when the signal flashed to turn
Left at the apartments because
He knew what that babysitter did
Before his seven-hour shift expired.
Now I can tour the ninety-nine test sites
Of Yucca Flat, hear the anecdotal
Evidence of poisoning dismissed.
Now the theory of hormesis says
Chernobyl will save lives, condition
The Russians like an invisible coach.
And now I'm offering one story
About pathfinding, how I learned
The clues of crossed sticks, the secrets
Of stones arranged into landmarks
In the manual I memorized,
The troop so far ahead nothing
Of them remained but symbols.
Now I'm learning the Roerich sign,
Three dots triangular in
A circle to protect against
Destruction. I'm turning wishful
Among hex signs for caution
Of every degree, something like
The tripled sticks or stones which warn
Comprehensively of danger:
Quicksand, cliff, poison ivy, wasps--
Simplicity's hope, not the demands
Of perpetual poison, something
Cartographers of the toxic need
For the long trip to the future.
Fifty thousand years, durable
As plastic, their signs must signify
The shriek of STOP. Reconvened,
The Voyager Committee tests
Symbols for flying to aliens

At the far end of half-lives.
Consider them children, they're told,
Who find inexplicable etchings;
Consider them Scouts who would flee
The permanent gesture for danger.
Or else they will gather for the slow
Levering of rock, the unscrewing
Of threads, waiting to see what will
Be lifted to the light, what might scream
Through the noise of insects, the shifting
Of dust, the chatter of elements
Emitted from a billion tongues
Like legacy's Esperanto.

Schmaltz

My mother's old bacon grease filled a jar
That sat among flour and sugar and salt
As if that unlabeled glass held one more
Kitchen staple. 100% fat,
100% thrift--the smoked flavor
Worked its way into eggs so we could eat
More meatless breakfasts. Or no eggs at all,
Just that grease, with green onions, reheated.
That meal took timing, taking the rye bread
To the barely hardened, sopping up *schmaltz*
Like uncles who drank coffee to cut it.
Such richness stayed overnight in the mouth
Where German melted into the English
Of memory, its sentimental schmaltz.
People my age were forgetting the waltz,
The fox-trot, and my father's sad box step.
What would be left, my mother worried, when
Conventional dances were gone? When thrift
Was laughed at? And all those warnings about
Salt and fat, the satisfaction of grease?
Already there were complaints about Heinz,
The soups my uncles made. Pittsburgh was home,
Now, to high blood pressure and heart disease,
All the Germans fleeing to the suburbs
Where bacon was drained, salt never slathered
On the crisped skin of chickens. My mother
Said we could shimmy it off in no time,
Doing the Twist and the Mashed Potato,
The dances of the slim who'd never heard
Of real *schmaltz* and the terrible success
Of learning place, those who wouldn't admit
To grandfathers who ate pure grease and lived,
Who'd punched in for fifty years and carried
The company's gold watch to prove it.

The Terrors

A house cleaned will be visited,
A house unkempt will live alone.
My mother, during the week, ended
Her stories in sorrow; my aunt,
On weekends, finished hers with fear:
The little boy's house got so dirty,
The neighbors burned it to the ground.
Outside were Stalin and the Rosenbergs,
The out-of-work and drunk, and those who
Suffered the great sin of shiftlessness.
There was a boy who saddened his mother
So often she turned into rain.
There was a boy who slept so much,
His mother buried him alive.
Outside was school where I'd follow
Directions or else, remember the maps
They had drawn and scaled for my walking.
A boy, once, had to live in a box
Because he forgot his way home from school.
A lost boy, at last, grew skinny
As straw and blew into a fire.
In the world of regret and anger,
Each of the women who waited
For me in first grade and day camp,
In Sunday School and the houses
Where music was taught by the half hour,
Had stories about boys who failed.
And so what? If I could read them,
They weren't about me; if every
Student could recite them, they were
No different than news, only public,
What the lettered world notices,
Not the personal, the terrors
We know variously in our hearts.

The Spiritualists

On television, this evening, stories
Of premature births, an astonishment
Of medical miracles, the problems
Which follow--children crippled, babies
Precarious with pneumonia, deaths
Of the weakest, like the son of a friend
Who showed slides, one night, each of them
Seconds apart in sequence during
The first day of a forty-hour life.
He spoke for himself and his silent wife,
Explained complications and symptoms,
The inevitability of loss.
And the last of those pictures, a head shot,
Stayed through his story of heaven,
How families were reunited,
Keeping me quiet about the woman
Who painted the face of a lost infant
On her breast, who sat in a cabinet
In the dark and waited for parents
To accept the possibility
Of contact. Who spoke to the departed.
Who bared the beautiful face
Of their dead child and thrust it through
The shadowed, sized opening
Into the dim light for viewing. Who asked
Joyful parents to extend their hands
To brush the soft faces of their children,
Repeating the name of the resurrected,
What I couldn't do, even then,
Staring at the lost, cyanotic child,
Thinking of reassurances,
The roll calls for the briefly living,
What sends us back to simple light.

Light Enough to be Lifted

Each evening, after dinner, from April
To October, my neighbor weeds his lawn
By hand. So it's perfect, he says,
Chemical-free, throwing one arm toward
Three treated lawns we face. I keep trim,
He says, by stepping outside before drinks
Or dessert, and he leaves me to sum the pounds
He's never added through the discipline
Of hands in the soil, to think of the woman
Who aborted her fetus so she'd be
Light enough to be lifted to heaven
During the Rapture. Of the man who built
A life-sized Jesus from toothpicks, counting
The square, the round, the flat and sandwich kinds
To sixty-five thousand separate sticks.
What weight of needs we carry. What fat so
Difficult to trim we butcher ourselves
With beliefs. I look down where the first thread
Of plantain might show itself, imagine
Seed and spore, the tangle of conception.
Below the earth, in Texas, this country
Has stored thirty-two billion cubic feet
Of helium. Just in case. Starting with
The threat, once, of possible blimp warfare,
Continuing through the astonishing
Catastrophes of the surface which lifts
As if the Rapture for inanimates
Were beginning, all the beautiful things
Soaring toward the heaven for possessions.

From THE TECHNOLOGY OF PARADISE
(1998)

Hanging the Pigs

*"During the middle ages there were dozens
of murder trials against animals."*

For murder, it was always
The domesticated, pigs
Especially, the ones who
Trampled children, danced their hooves
Through memory's red seizure.

Or the pigs, sometimes, were tortured,
Squealed clear confessions of guilt.
And locked in solitary,
They grunted the black mass prayer,
Snuffled to the devil's sleep,
So closely guarded, so bound,
None of those killers escaped.

And when they trotted, back-whipped,
To trial, a few of those pigs,
According to the records,
Had court-appointed lawyers
To plead the victim-defense,
The mental-deficiency
Gambit, none of it moving
The men who stood in for God.

So all were executed—
Hammered, butchered—and some led
To the gallows, snouts sliced off,
Wearing white human masks, dressed
In coats and trousers, lifted
To the bleating, back-legged stance
Of the hell-pentecost, all
The silenced crowd pressed forward,
Waiting for those pigs to hang,
Shutting up their Satan tongues.

The Cabinet of Wonders

Frederick Ruysch, the great embalmer, could fill all the veins and arteries, none ruptured, before his solution hardened.

From Finders, Keepers

So expert, finally, at perfecting
Preservation, Ruysch worked with capillaries,
With filling the fine vessels of the face
So well these infants' heads in bottles float
Eyes open, as if surface still mattered.
Here, in this jar, an arm rising from lace
To grip an eye socket centuries old.
Here, a skull vented for a view of the brain.
Here, the small skeleton which holds a mayfly
To remind us of transience those mornings
When the *wunderkammer* of sickness takes
All the available space with the keepsakes
Of pain, the curios for fever, and
The repeated mementoes of wheezing.

In this museum in which we love ourselves,
The dispassionate fetus will not break
Its stare. Severed at the neck, we know, yet
Ruysch's daughter sewed the lace for its throat,
Selected beads; and sometimes she helped him clothe
His allegorical tableaux, fetal
Skeletons walking and weeping and playing
The violin with a dried-artery bow.

Geology of kidney stones, botany
Of blood vessels and lungs, intestine snakes
(Though the wonder is we need these warnings)
Which slither up from the fields to wrap these bones—
I've listened to "possible mass" after
One of those landscape kidney stones doubled
Me down to emergency. I've posed for
Tableaux with CAT-Scan and seen myself exposed
On the bulletin board for death, so many

Patients waiting in those subdivided rooms
We could have formed our own tableaux for fear,
A full *kunstkammer* where the conditions
Of our bodies could have been curated
To display the memory absolutions.

Whatever Ruysch is saying now, these rooms are
Weaving me inside. In the hypothesis
Of the Stendahl Syndrome, some tourists grow
Giddy after art. Their pulse accelerates.
They sweat and faint, or hallucinate, some
Of them depressed, some euphoric, some of them
Omnipotent in their hearts, though so many
Of these displays have been lost I can only
Trace the outline of every suspect organ
I can locate, running my fingers along
The perimeter of the liver to feel
For exactly what I never want to find.
Although as soon as I think this, I say
Of course not, how silly, like the doctor
Who, when I insisted I could distinguish
One kidney heavier than the other,
Shook his head sadly and said "impossible."

The Doctrine of Signatures

The woman who followed me from flower
To flower said Birthday? Anniversary?
And I shook my head among the arrangements
Until she shifted to Accident? Sickness?
Guiding and pointing and introducing
The Doctrine of Signatures, how all plants
Were created to serve us, their powers
To cure revealed by shape, by size, by shade:
The bloodshot blossoms of the eyebright
Heal pinkeye; the Chinese lantern plant
Is bladder-shaped for stones. Paracelsus,
She said, acknowledging the source, adding
Yellow plants for the liver, ginseng root
For general malaise, prescriptions
So simple we could arrange eternity
In a greenhouse if we knew the shapes
Of our weakest parts, my mother's heart
Winding down while I thought of petals
Red and sugared as a lover's gift.
And since then I've comparison-shopped
For pancreas, thyroid, lymph glands, walking
The aisles with such ignorance of form
I might as well choose a shape for the soul—
Lilac, lily, morning glory—as if
Resurrection could be watered and fed
While we search for the flowers which form
Like tumors, the buds which open into
The ominous mass on the x-ray,
And the seeds or spores that are scattered
Like great seasonings for the earth, blended
So perfectly they lie invisible
Until they rise from our astonished tongues.

The Throne of the Third Heaven of the National Millenium General Assembly

With Old Testament prophets on the left hand,
With New Testament disciples to the right,
The design sung by the angels visiting
Washington, crooning to James Hampton, who built
A throne room for the second coming of Christ.
With aluminum foil, with kraft paper,
With the gold glitter of packagining for wine
And cigarettes and chocolate candy.
With all of the thirteen years the public schools
And my parents worked to make me worth saving,
He formed cardboard and plywood to prepare
A ceremonial setting for the Lord.
With insulation board. With desk blotters.
With failed light bulbs and outcast jelley jars.
With the inventory of the dumpster,
The fervor of finding each object holy.
With dedication. With faith. With cold and heat.
With sickness and fatigue. With the minutes
Someone else formed foil into a planet
Of scraps. With the hours someone else spooled thread
Into an enormous ball. With the late nights
I worked with my father in his bakery
To form bread and cake from a million fragments.

With matched icons to attract the gold bolt
Of Christ's descent while I dreamed the glitter stars
Of success, the bright As of achievement,
And couldn't build anything with my hands
Except stacks of books. With calluses
While I wanted to be the film aliens
Who moved objects with their minds, stacked our army's
Poised weapons as a first line of defense.
With mild oaths while I parried the fists
Of classmates who walked the halls with failure's fever,
Laying their hot hands flush to my honors face.
With original prayers and hymns sung

To the great God of imminent return
While all the lyrics I loved turned tumescent
With lust, each melody smoking cigarettes,
Drinking beer, and loving the pinball of sequins
And lamé; while all the verses wanted
Breasts and thighs, and I brought a thousand pop
Records into my room where returning Jesus
Would find me memorizing the simple chords
For desire and angst, repeating them like litanies
I heard twice a week from my family's pew.

With anthems and cantatas. With chanted creeds.
With the beatitudes of blessed are
The builder's hands, blessed is the throne room
Formed with the refuse of temporary rule,
Blessed are those who believe in the sweet voice
Which whispers *yes*. Now, James Hampton was telling
Himself in 1964, Christ will strip
This warehouse roof, open this dazzling throne room.
Now, the gathering of souls will shield their eyes
And blink through the final state of the union
Address in heaven's bifigured conference room.
Now, I echoed, packing for college, taking
What I wanted from my gilded room, leaving
With clothes, with trophies, with every record
I warbled with the Robins, with the Blue Jays,
With the Orioles, Ravens, and Cardinals
Through the bifigured world of A and F,
Crew cut and duck tail, pen and fists; each record
Replayed by lifting the needle, placing it
Where pop and crackle siganlled the second
Before harmonies began, never thinking
Of Hampton unlocking the door to glory,
Retracing its symmetry to the drawstring
Of the bare light bulb above the golden throne.
The Dream of Alchemy

After one novocain needle, after another,
My tongue turning idiot through assurance, I read
That the cremated poison the air. Kidney damage,
Neurological harm--what escapes up the chimney,
Vaporized, is mercury, twenty-four pounds a year.

On average. Per oven. From silver fillings like
The six I have, one of them driving me, this morning,
To be shot to slurring. And right here, next paragraph,
The dangers of zealous chewing, how metal might reach
The brain when we attack corn, caramel, or well-done steak.

I multiply half a gram times six, my weighted share,
Search the chart for consequences of the dentist's chair.
Unlikely, it says, or rare, but the dentist returns,
And she's wearing a mask, pulling on gloves to protect
Herself from the evils in splattering spit and blood.

I slow breathe, count chrysanthemums outside the window.
I hear the sieved sounds of "fracture" and "rinse," thud my tongue
Away from the alloyed pins. "We'll give this a few weeks
To settle down," she says, unmasking, "then it's time for
Your first gold crown." So I bob my head, reading her smile

Like an alien caught at the border, smiling, too,
Sitting up while she tells me about the costs of crowns
And procedures while I think of the missed incentives
For care, one sixth of my mercury gone, enough years
Left, most likely, for five more fractures, sufficient heat

To billow the brilliance from an insulated flue
As if the transmutation of the body began
In the dream of alchemy, that cloud releasing mist
So fine and brief its redeemable promise will coat
The living with an unseen, yet ambiguous sheen.

From INVENTING ANGELS
(1994)

-

A Murder of Crows

Driving home, I see all of them
By the highway, pecking at
Whatever is splayed out and torn,
And none of them flutter up
Or hop deeper on the shoulder.
The houses start to thicken,
The one set back from the road owned
By a woman who has been
Moved upstate for care. At the light,
I turn slowly and hear nothing
Promising in the noise the brakes
Make, how they remind me they
Will eventually fail, but
The man who lives next door says
He has a book for me downstairs,
And I have to watch him limp
Toward the dark, thinking how little
I read. I could stammer that
Words are ineffective as skin,
But I follow him and see
His cellar ceiling-high with books.
"Seventy-thousand," he says,
Nodding at the fire-hazard piles
Of them. We smile together
Though the room is impassable,
And I know I will never
Open the volume he hands me,
Vanity Fair, his seventh
Garage-sale copy, and I could
Repeat, "A labor of mules,
A drift of hogs," tell him about
The collective nouns for things,
How names can amuse us and do
Nothing to change this evening,
Whether the weight of this novel
Impresses me or he will
Follow it with others, stacking
Them in my arms and never
Imagining I could drop them.

The Book of Numbers

Using a standard typewriter, Marva Drew, from 1968 to 1974, typed the numbers
from 1 to 1,000,000 on 2,500 pages.

From *The Best of the Worst*

Fat with ambition, this book,
Though you can see how its plot
Must progress regularly
As wills in the careful scripts
Of scriveners. In this tale,
Everything says conclusion.
Each symbol, each myth predicts
A sort of Rapture when life
Goes blank as an end page, all
Of the story well-planned as
An Earth-centered universe.
I want, tonight, to say I've
Started that book of numbers
So often I think it's mine.
At least to a thousand, where
I've stopped; or once, ten thousand,
A weekend with childhood flu,
My aunt hauling the pages
Downstairs to ponder. "You got
Every number right," she said,
Reporting like proofreaders.
Ten thousand and one, I thought,
Ten thousand and two, and went
Outside, after that fever,
To bounce a ball off the roof,
Off the wall, to simulate
One tense game in a season
Of one hundred-fifty-four.
And in ten years, if one group
Of believers is correct,
The world will explode because
That year matches the number
Of weeks Jesus walked the world.

The next year, too, will shatter
Us, a famous psychic claims,
And then the year 2000
Will send millions of hopeful
Up the mountains to welcome
The universal blindness.
So we need someone to count,
Take on a second volume
To insure we don't know how
It all turns out. "Pass it on,
No returns," we say, schoolboys
Punching the arms beside us.
Or circled, Boy Scouts, around
A campfire: "Jack still burning,"
Puffing on a glowing stick,
Handing it off before it
Goes black. One million and one,
Marva, one million and two . . .

Inventing Angels

1

Let us explain, the church said, the mystery
Of the inexplicable bones. One: God ran tests,
What did we think? There's always waste—to get
Eden right, He had to fail a thousand times,
All those bones the rejected prototypes
For paradise. Two: God, for personal
Reasons, don't ask, created fossils. Wouldn't
You use omniscience for deceit? Wouldn't
You test your people with the illusion
Of previous life? Three: There were species
Too late for the ark, the animals at fault,
Indifferent to "All aboard." A pair
Of mammoths dawdled; the pterodactyls waffled;
Noah had enough to do with rationing,
With teaching the Peaceable Kingdom precepts.

2

Or Noah, we guessed, senses that ark too small.
Afraid to blame God for the stupid specs,
He discreetly left half the world behind.
On Sundays, we learned the revised standard
Version of his story from a flannel board.
We followed felt cutouts through Noah's journey;
We heard reports on each Ararat attempt,
The church or celebrities funding those climbs
For the ark's splinters on the favorite
Mountain of the faithful. And we imagined
That cloth reshaped to everything preserved
By lava or tar whenever our teacher
Fast-forwarded to old Abraham and
The near-sacrifice he made following
The next audible orders from God.

3

The aurochs, quagga, great auk, and moa—
In the heresy of the backward glance,

An astonishment of passenger pigeons
Blackens the sky. One bird, its eyes sewn shut,
Is tied by hunters to a stool. And it calls
Loudly, of course, from the dark, drawing the flock
To the pogrom until nothing remains
But gangsters' slang, how we've used the dodo,
Which posed for artists, stood still for butchers,
The intent of predators bred from its genes.
What lasts? What lasts? A hundred years after
It disappeared, the flightless dodo turned
To hoax: Because there were no skeletons.
Because portrait art was weak evidence
Against the circumstantial disbelief.

4

The immediate doubt of the witness—
In each museum we read to verify
The bones, even those with hides or feathers
Like Martha, the last passenger pigeon,
Who was caged in the Cincinnati Zoo,
Who died and was not buried and rose again
As exhibit a year after Moreschi,
The last *castrato*, retired. The labels
On each of his ten recordings call him
The Soprano of the Sistine Chapel,
The church confessing to the altered truth
Of its soloists, inventing angels
We can visualize by listening
To the museum's gramophone, rapt with hearing
The pure, unnatural voice of extinction.

The Wonder Children

His parents posed beside him, the latest
Child prodigy, thirteen, is tonight's good news.
He's entering medical school, puberty,

And the reporter is pleased to predict,
To say many of us will be grateful
For the certainty of his surgeon's hands.

Doogie Howser, she tries, citing sitcom
As if it were history, counting on
Most of us to know her network's lineup,

Though she could mention a hundred children
Sure with scalpels, repeat Mozart, Mill,
And Henry Truman Safford. Or tell us

The Willy Sidis story, not optioned
To television, not yet—his entering
Harvard, eleven years old; his leaving

Learning behind, saying *no* to lectures
And libraries with a self-inflicted
Resignation. How he adopted the broom

And mop. How his hands welcomed the scythe,
Stacked the streetcar transfers he treasured.
How he died, forty-six, in a rented room,

Outliving a host of precocious children:
Cardiac, master of languages, dead
At seven; the Infant of Lubeck,

The Bible's index, expired at four, each
A wonder child forever. And another
Mapped the only route to the needle's-eye

Entrance to heaven. Calculated the miles,
Established the angle of ascension.
And left the precise point of departure

For some future child genius to figure.
Including the rate of change for all things,
Their positions within the shifting sky

To one thousandth of a second as we
Revolve and spin, as each location in
The universe simultaneously moves.

Like our moon, we know, which is spiraling
Away from earth, and, in a million years,
Will be too distant to eclipse the sun.

Oxygen

Somebody is always struggling with oxygen
Like Mrs. Oppenlander this summer, even
The memory of the word blocked as she recollects
Instead the boy I was when these tubes were elsewhere.
"How thin," visitors might say, "how precarious,"
As if adjectives were appropriate along
Highland Avenue, all of the houses built before
The atomic scare, all of them turning to gray
Because they are older than I am—my clumsy
Logic, my noticing that the street-bed bricks are
The same pale ones I painted with water colors
That August when lightning struck the steeple next door.

Thirty-seven, and I have returned to this street
Of lost breath where lung after lung fills like wineskins;
All of these stairs, all of these hot bedrooms carved out
Of tight attics that look out toward the dormant tracks.
How height deceives; how thirty years ago I stood
Upstairs and felt myself plunging to the sidewalk;
How we surprise ourselves and expect to mumble
"Where am I?" as the ordinary evening fills
With mucus, strangling after it lies down to sleep.

This could be the road where my children have listened
To their thin neighbor cough until he disappeared
The way Greismere Street climbs above my grandfather's
Sold and remodeled house, the first turn frightening
The flatlanders who visit, running the blind curve
Chance right onto the slick cobblestones, right along
The cliff's edge narrow lane where no one thought of cars
That could plummet into Etna like UFOs,
All shrieks and shattering glass—the mauve confusion,
The two-tiered Möbius Strip of it carrying
Everybody back to his beginning, down from
The highest house where Fleischers, both unsteady from
The saw of surgery, watch the borough shrivel,
Talk of their new neighbors who erected a huge,

Brilliant cross at Christmas and drove off into
A holiday toll accident. "It's the thin air,"
They insist. "It's the leaning back into the slope
That disturbs balance and makes us gasp," and I add
A damp spring excuse for all of this breathless luck.

The Butterfly Effect

If a butterfly flaps its wings in Brazil, it might produce a tornado in Texas.
From *The Laws of Chaos*

Early in the newsmagazine
These Haitian women are wailing,
And those who are not are holding
Their breath and the hands of men
Tense with a bullet expectation.
And I've read, too, that the wind
Tonight may have originated
From their mourning, the beating
Of their arms in the air sending
This record warm front north.
I've read about fractals,
The Russian Dolls of the universe,
Diamonds made of diamonds made
Of diamonds diminishing in size;
I've learned the Butterfly Effect,
How chaos is not chaos,
How some slaughter in Haiti flaps
Its wings and churns into my grip
On the arm of my son, my clenched teeth
And hiss as he flutters his free arm
And wails and changes the future
Of weather in a country east of us
Where a father will choose, he thinks,
To stun his son to obedience.
And when I leave him to let the dog
Walk me into sense, the unnatural wind
Chatters the branches that skitter her
To a barking panic on our street
Of sculpted shrubbery where Christmas bulbs,
In one yard, might be arranged
Into language if you're properly
Angled, upstairs, across the street,
Positioned like an antenna straining
For a distant station, my son in his window

Watching me handle the dog, my breath
Without its winter clouds, nothing he'd believe
Could join the southern grief of a warm front.

The Theories for Ball Lightning

Mr. Smink told us the history of the high school band,
Which boys had fainted in parades, which girls had soloed
To applause. We smeared "Camptown Races," blatted
"Yankee Doodle"; Mr. Smink explained how our music
Traveled through space, how it would play forever
On a frequency someone green might hear. Lately,
He'd been spiraling from seniors to fourth-graders,
Repeating FACE and Every Good Boy Deserves Fudge
As if Martians might love mnemonics. After us
Were third-graders with rental horns, second-graders
With tonettes, but he picked us to tell how
His friend had been killed by music, his radio
Plunging into the tub when he reached for soap.

We understood nobody would die for the songs
We were practicing, but we wanted to fill
A bathtub, tip someone's Philco into the water
While "Sugartime" or "Tammy" was on the air,
Zapping one horror on the launch pad. We hoped
There'd be lightning, some Shazam! bolt of weather
In the locked bathroom. We asked Mr. Smink
If the electrocuted glowed, and he told us
About the woman who claimed a cloud of light
Pursued her, how she brushed its lecher's touch
From her arm and it exploded. We finished
"Oh, Susanna." We blew our spit on the wooden floor
And listened to Mr. Smink recite the theories
For ball lightning: Bubbles of burning methane;
Swarms of glowing pollen; throngs of electrified gnats—
As if that woman had eaten badly before the attack,
Bringing a visit from an electronic Marley's ghost,
Something like seeing the luminous crews who piloted
Their saucers transfixed by our beginners' tunes.

The Skill of the Sunlight's Good

The miracle animals approach, creep
Forward like the Ugandan Tortoise,
Who talked from his shell, or leap
Like Chris, the Psychic Dog, barking
Futures. They nod, paw, tap hooves—
And Lady Wonder, the Telepathic Horse,
Put her nose on oversize keys to print
Fortunes. What typos to hunt and peck;
She nudged and pressed, prophecy if you
Bought "The Skull of the Sinlight's Goof."
She could have been an economist,
Could have run for office and dictated
Letters to secretaries hired to follow
The mute inflections of her grammar.

Which of us scoffs? We won't harm anyone
With an ESP for heaven, mouthing hymns,
Chanting phrases of faith. There were weeks
I memorized Bible verses, recited them
At the altar, and I wasn't crippled.
This week I've sung "The Old Rugged Cross"
And repeated the standard prayer
Of the church aloud. And in public.
After I said "Amen," a child I'd known
Was off to burial. So be it.
So the animals use four legs forward
And do wonderful things if we let
Our mouths open to the old words of snort
And bark and nicker, saying, "Of course."

The Congestive Failure of Belief

For the first minute, it's a nightmare
House-loose, someone finally solving
The locked doors, someone dissatisfied
With the stereo and silverware
And drifting down the hall for bodies.

After midnight, in my own unease
With sleep, I'd been brooding down a list
Of reunion ills: the permanent
Ink of age, how watered values freeze
On the crust of my winter visit.

I'd had an hour, like always, to think
Behind the double dark of closed eyes;
I'd listened to my father below
In his basement reluctant to sink
Into the end of this holiday.

He'd spent all his meal talk on death, cash
Saved by sudden's undemanding care.
Insurance, he'd said, stocks, deeds, a will,
Nothing he'd mentioned before, a wash
Of worry in the familiar wine.

Below freezing, the barometer
Bleating snow-to-come, I need to drive
East before the weather enters town,
And now the new noise outside the door,
Not my father, who never rises

At night, not the familiar terror
Of stealth that demands light and voices.
In the dark, my breathing, my mother's,
Her doubled pace of mine a mirror
For the rhythms that will slow us all.

She is standing in the black of pause
As if I've choked and gone blue-quiet
In the cowboy's room across from hers,
And I listen in return because
I might measure the scars on her heart.

The congestive failure of belief.
She drops forty years in her stillness,
Sentry for crib death, come to lift me
To the reflexive noun for relief,
Clutched to her flow and gone to feeding.

Every Reachable Feather

On Sundays, now, my youngest son completes
His confirmation schooling, has me check
The answers for his Bible-study homework:

Besides Jesus, who rose from the dead?
He's written Lazarus like the workbook
Wants, but I suggest figurative Jonah,

The fortunate falls of Adam and Eve,
Confusing my son and recalling
How a neighbor, dead this week, hated

His wife's parrot for its squawking echo.
Look at my snake, he'd say. Never a noise.
Hardly a mess. And he set that boa

Loose to coil around the parrot's cage.
That quiets it, he'd say, and finally
The parrot went mute, his wife complaining

It was crazy, that parrots who utter
Nothing are depressed, and I agreed
Because every reachable feather

Was gone. If it had hands, she told me,
It would have plucked its head, and I said,
"It looks like food," just before my neighbor

Wrapped his fat arms around the cage, pressed
His face to the bars as if he didn't
Fear for his eyes. There was madness,

The constrictor coiling as it must,
The parrot suffocating in the dark,
Reviving, reviving again,

A home-bound record for resurrection,
Plucked and crazed and skittering back to
The vacant eternity of owners.

How to Verify God

By weighing the soul, putting the dying
On the sensitive scale we need
For balance: Someone, in 1907, did this,
A doctor who had access to death,
Those who could not refuse, and he
Measured one less ounce in those corpses,
Imagining flight as the beam dropped.

Well, I was glad to read about McDougall,
How faith, for once, can be shored up
By science, though there were plenty of hoots,
The kind I heard for being a Boy Scout,
An acolyte, a safety patrol captain,
All of them requiring a uniform
That made every thug in Pittsburgh jeer.

Over and over I had to walk Route 8
Where the trailer court made boys
Wear studs, where Pine Creek flooded
Each spring until nothing but poverty
Was left. I wanted a gun; I wanted
To watch all those sneering obscenities
Tumble back into the sewer of that creek—
What dark hands would instruct me;
What teacher, always a woman, would replace
My bandages with the silk touch of desire?

My cousin died. I lugged him
By one chrome handle and would not admit
The ache in my arm. My uncle died,
And I struggled with that stranger,
Taking one sixth of him across Sharp's Hill,
Which will never be flooded, and that day
I could see how the mill's soot lay lower
Than us, caught in the valley by inversion.
That was my last pall-bearing. Our family's
Heavy Pittsburgh breath held while

I outgrew that duty, but I read later
That McDougall tested dogs, control group
For the soul, that he thought conversions
Would follow. Waiting was the hardest part,
Wishing for weight loss. There were times
When McDougall watched the chest of each man,
Sure this magic flew from the heart.
There was a blur, he thought, when the body
Lightened; the dogs, of course, lost
Nothing, the air around their dying still.

From THE DOUBLE NEGATIVES OF THE LIVING
(1992)

Naming the Sky

"There's my sky," my father says. I don't know
What he expects, answer, in his driveway,
"It's clear, all right," and idling in neutral,
Think he's planning to tell me the ancient
Names for the dots or the tales they fathered,
People who suffered, changed, and ascended
While somebody handed their stories down.
Two dippers and Orion—I forget
The rest or never learned or failed to see
Anything but the stars scattered on our scale
Of pulse and breath. I want him to show me
Archer, bear, lion; I want marble busts
Of myth to form above us like pillars
Of flame, chariots of fire, accounting
For every light, and because my mother
Has died, wonder if he means to show me
Where she is, how one cluster has reformed
To suggest a melodrama of hope.
Heavy-headed with travel, I wait while
The time-released light, set to eleven,
Blinks off in his living room like stars near
The horizon tumbling off the sky's screen.
And I remember no clock in this house
Is correct, all six set so fast no one
Would believe them, early as wet robins
In today's false thaw of February.
We stand with the night in our lungs; we breathe
A sentence of silence until he says,
"Venus and Jupiter," directs me low
In the sky where I see so many lights
I can nod, certain they are among them.

The Flower Remedies

1

"Are flowers thinking?" my son asked once.
"Do they know who we are?" and I worried
For his manhood, wished he'd requested
A translation for snarls, the idioms
Of growls. "They know us like the newly born,"
I told him. "If they breathed, they would cry."

2

Nothing could keep Edward Bach from flowers.
Not scoffing. Not weather. Not the symptoms
He showed when he approached the proper plants:
Hatred near holly; beside mustard, gloom.
So sensitive, Bach was, he imagined
Self-pity by chicory; guilt at pine.
They healed him, healed the distress of others
Who drank his flower teas. Take cerato
For self-doubt; taste iris for frustration;
Then smile, sip aspen for anxiety,
Whisper, "Bach," say, "The Flower Remedies."

3

I hear my wife say her student, today,
Sat up barking, and she thought, like her class,
He was joking, a first-day-of-school-test
For his teacher. "He was growling," she says.
"He sounded so much a dog I thought it
Was talent." Under the table our Spitz
Lies listening to what it knows; already
I want to say "Well?" but my wife offers
The syndrome's name for bad luck in the genes.
Snarl, spit, what the old exorcists knew.
Our dog waits to sit and beg, but no one
Is holding food. The house trick it's mastered—
Not to be deceived by one thing at least,
Thinking in barks and growls like a student.

4

To believe in the brain's
Many routes from disease;
To learn stress buffers;
To read this week's book
On meditation, stretching,
Deep breathing and joy.
"Rock rose for panic, gorse
For despair"—each day is
Pocked with moods; what we
Become has walked in others
And still we study. Choler,
We read—bile, phlegm, blood—
So medieval in another
Smug week of solutions.

5

I am walking to work, thinking of flowers. How few I recognize. The
roadside is littered with mysteries, and I know as little about the cars that
brush my walking. I need a lesson in America, in goods, in the names
for constructed things, and I say, "Cerato, iris, aspen" to begin the multi-
plication of forgetfulness. I would turn into these fields if I remembered
the identity clues—color, shape, pattern, number—everything leaves
and petals, each of my terrors swept away by the undertow of flowers.

The Stuttering Cures

One thing we learn: how much poison
The body can take. Alcohol,
For instance. Cruelty. Prayer as duty.
Once a day Ronnie Muller read
History aloud because Mrs. Cook
Demanded a paragraph
Of recitation. Stuttering's cure,
Perhaps, though Ronnie Muller,
Force-fed like a protest faster,
Never finished a sentence
Before P or T swallowed
His breath and the carburetor
In his throat stalled for good.

And always, there's worse, some surgeon
A hundred years before Mrs. Cook who
Snipped portions of stutterers' tongues,
Clipped strategic bits and pieces
Like speech therapy's barber.

All of those stories of stutterers
Who can sing, who can whisper,
Who can perfectly speak in unison
Or when they cannot hear themselves:
Each one of those patients, after
The plastic surgery for speech,
Waited for that doctor to unwrap
His transformed tongue, to say, "Yes, now,"
As welcome. Think of that first
Tentative stutter, the patient
Hearing imperfection's nuance,
The misery of misdirected breath
Lengthening to the wish for
The speechless life of stone.
So easily, the wind we've stored
Scatters the memos of our thinking.
The man who sold me insurance

Lost his tongue to cancer, entered
The enormous stammer of silence,
The messages on his note pad
Thinning to *yes* and *no*, to tapping,
At last, on the empty tablet,
Nothing anyone could decipher,
As if it were a personal code
Or all his thoughts now stuttered.

Reaching the Deaf

Screams of distress are in the vocal spectrum least affected by age deterioration.
from *Extraordinary Endings*

I've cursed behind my mother,
Spent my rage-list of phrases
While she scrubbed grease from plates.
My father, now, hears nothing
On his right, and I've tested him
With blasphemy from the shotgun seat.
And I've settled, full front,
For vague heresies, measured
My lies by volume, but here is
The news of Gertrude Jameison,
Eighty-five, harassing
Doug Thompson forty-six years,
Calling him eight times a day
Despite court orders, four months
At a penal farm, and a lock
On her phone. Nothing's stopped her.
Not a stroke. Not confinement
In a nursing home. Not Thompson
Gone so silent on the line
She asks if he knows her, if he
Has something to say, shrill
With still guessing the phrase
To stop his heart. Some screams
Must run the painted needle to
The North of the penny compass.
Some distress must sing itself
Up the noon or midnight
Of the gumball clock. Think of
The way a woman calls and calls;
How another waters her lawn
All day for a year, swamping
Herself and her neighbors, what
She means to say in her faucet,
The sum of her language forming

A shrieking wetlands. Think how
The pulse of imminence searches
Through things in common, speeding us to
The bestial vowels that reach the deaf.

Six Kinds of Music, the Wallpaper of Breasts

I thought I'd drive the seventy miles
To see my son, slouch in a dorm room
With six kinds of music, the pleasure
Of his wallpaper of breasts. His wild hair
Was jammed down his shirt; we said nothing while
We breathed together as he looked for shoes
And I thumbed through his college catalogue
As if it were *People* at the dentist.

I recognized Tom Petty, Prince, The Who.
I heard, when another door swung open,
The Fine Young Cannibals, and I could have
Asked my son who else was singing along
That hall, but he said, finally, "That guy
On the cover was arrested for rape,"
And I closed his core curriculum, looked
Again at the student in the sweatshirt,
The name of my son's school across his chest
To sell parents, because he was seated
In the stacks, a sense of scholarship.

I felt like the fool of the worthless deed,
The lunkhead of the nosedived junk bond.
That student's slick smile had beamed at us
Through a senior year of choices; I'd tried
To read the titles of the books bunched on
The shelf behind him and made jokes about
The fabricated pose of study, how
Two hundred catalogues we owned had been
Cloned like the white pillars, ivy, and
The quarter-hour chorus of carillons.

I wasn't sure what it meant to have
A rapist on that cover, see my son
In his sweatshirt across the lawn from
Where a new library was being built.
For all I knew, the girl lived in that dorm,

Had a copy of this catalogue
Among her books. "He's history," I heard.
"He's expelled." And one of the stereos,
At least, was softened, turned off, or the door
Of its owner's room was so unlikely
Thick it shut the sound inside like a hand
Insistent over an astonished mouth.

The Double Negatives of the Living

After the pastor spoke well,
After he opened our route
With syntax and grammar
Correct as his manner,
I could follow my mother
To her grave and lapse into
The double negatives
Of the living. I could talk
Two hours past midnight with
My father in the steelworker
Idiom of his city, hearing
The fried mush of morning,
The white Sunday silence,
The many tongues of the cross
Speaking dialect stories
Of the holy mill. I could catch
His punctuation by breath born
In the thick ash of evening,
Overhear the end stops in
His coughs, the accidental case
For the thrift store's stock,
The body's swift tumors;
The chance of modifiers
For the factory uncles,
The fat, baking aunts,
The grandmothers in the pews
Of their dead husbands
Or rocking on porches
Flush with the brutal streets.
And finally the commas for
Steel, rivers, bridges, bars.
And Christ, the Expletive,
And all of the language
Of the land that we leave
And return to, reopening
The earth and stammering

Like the past's twin-speech,
What we know by repeating,
What runs on without us.

From PLANT VOICES
(1991)

What the Builders Left

Some of them must have believed in symbols,
Leaving the refuse shaped just so, aligned
In arrows, pentangles, double daggers,
And one cross out back in the bulldozed mud
I'll be raking in April. Among them
Is a monolith of shale stuck upright
So no one would think accidents, and I
Warn my children, "Stay clear," while I study
The folklore threats of East Snyder County,
How these fifth generation Germans pass
Hatred through their tales, how page after page
Of phone book cousins say hemophilia,
Albino, and why did you relocate
Where builders make the time to form totems.
Someone named Kratzer restacked the lumber
In my living room; someone named Mengel
Snipped the wiring and bent it until fear
Drove sparks from mouth to tail. And whichever
Dunkleberger jammed this six-foot shale spear
Into this February mud must have
Shouted for help, must have wig-wagged his arms
In a convincing way to bring at least
Two simple cousins who were uneasy
With touching this hex there is no chant for.

Groaning Boards

In the Letters Section, the fundamentalists
Are talking about creation, how most readers'
Futures are fire. They're condensing antiquity,
Editing to verify Eden, and claiming
Carbon dating one more pitchfork brand on the soul.
"It's their diet," a friend laughs, handing me a plate,
His church-picnic food line so slow I examine
The broken barn across the highway, start thinking,
To pass time, I might witness its collapse into
One of those rubble piles you pass, anonymous
As all of these covered dishes, three-bean salads,
Scalloped potatoes, nothing noted until someone
Claims it's wood from an ark—Noah's, the Covenant's.
And I remember standing in these picnic lines
With plates as empty, searching for something to end
The embarrassment of taste. The congregation
Heaped cole slaw and baked beans, meat loaf and sauerkraut,
Macaroni, red beet eggs, joking, "It all goes
To the same place." It was the Lord's plenty; it was
America's riches incarnate while the coal
Trains' schedules thinned into broth, the mines sewn back up
And sealed like cancer patients. Nobody mentioned
Subsidence, though the road to those picnics was roped
By the varicose veins of tipped houses. I found
Applesauce, ham it took fifteen minutes to trim,
And watched the old women stand like Joe Palooka
Air bags, catch themselves with weight through their thighs, and raise
Their canes and walkers like weapons. They admonished
Their bodies like Kathryn Kuhlman broadcasts: "Heal me,
Lord, though I'm not worthy," they whispered, eighty years
Of hauling the fat of the land on their shoulders.
The lard coating of the past on their tongues, first formed
By German, brought up the phlegm of repetitive
Work with its old world cough of consonants. And here,
In Selinsgrove, it's God's Holiness Campground, horse
And buggy, the three hitching posts at Weis Market,
The translucent skull caps on two of the tellers

At Snyder County Trust, and one shrunken woman
At this feast who's dieting a tumor away,
Eating dried fruit and nuts to outlive her doctor.
She's up front with this year's examples; she's shaking
The golf ball out of her brain. When, some nights, I dream
Myself dead over cliffs, beside terrorist bombs,
In front of madmen's shotguns, the next scene is black;
I keep it to myself like fear of failure, but
This traditional food speaks from the long tables,
Insists on God as I joke with my friend who loads
His plate for both of us, fat and laughing about
My nostalgic Pittsburgh beer, about his cabbage
Soup diet abandoned after diarrhea.
And I remember, too, that some of those women
Were tied to chairs, nodded and swayed through those Sundays'
Second sermons, that I wandered, afterward, through
The faithful like an erosion gulley, feeling
The fishbarb snag of guilt hook my shirt from behind.
And likewise, after we eat, in that barn's darkness
My bored sons will grow quiet, paying attention
To a footfall of wind, retribution, using
Their sudden, bullhorn voices for balance, courage;
And in those groves at dusk, the oldest women would
Test themselves before waiting for hands to lift them.
All of those widows with humps would put prayer away
And limp to the taxis of their sons or nephews.
They believed wings could be latent in the spine's pain,
Patient as wisdom teeth, as breasts or beard or birth,
The rest of the body's redeemable promise.

Sleeping with the Leper

The Spider Behind Glass

Our heartbeats. We talk ourselves
Awake and listen to nothing
As we shrivel. The spider
Behind glass has opened his home.

We gather each shred of light.
Our room is rearranged until
The untouched dust of neglect
Is positioned for our feet.

We ought to move, percentages
Still with us. So slowly, we
Push ourselves up on elbows,
Concentrate on the padded risks
That are not entirely silent.

Remember, this is no insect.
There are eight ways to hear its
Eraser shuffle. We swallow
The syllables that rise, each
Nerve listening for evidence.

Centralia

Some places transform air
Into ash, every protest
Burned when it touches down.
Which is what 1000 degrees does,
These hot spots that glow
In the night drizzle.
We watch them the way
We inspect our fireplace
Before sleep. One ember
May sputter to the carpet

Like lottery-luck.
We buy no tickets;
We are boarding up worry;
We are overlooking
The row house connection
Of our arson-prone lives.

That's our neighborhood
Testing our walls. At Park
And Locust the cellar
Collapsed like a feeble coup,
All we see of politics.
That's the present metered
On our alarm: 35 parts
Per million sends a siren
Into our sleep because
We live over exhaust,
Because the hole for the hose
Shifts whenever whim grows bored.

Our canaries flutter
Like apprehension; nothing
Is sustained but cures:
How someone will shrink
Our tumors into power;
How he will heat our homes For 1000 years because
Niagara Falls tumbles
Underfoot . . .

December thins into
Our twenty-third year
Of this. Seen from above,
This constellation we
Walk on adds more detail,
Domestic animal feeding.

The field of hot spots

"One of us would steal a newspaper from a porch and we'd run back into the field of hot spots, crumpling the paper into basketball wads we'd shoot—jump hooks, three pointers from way outside—checking our scores off each time our pages would take flame when they landed, though we got too good and one afternoon Joey Augustine hit seven in a row from twenty feet, exploding a whole Sunday financial section so fast we got bored and just balled up the rest of what we had and heaved it. We gave it up after that, remembering that last quick whoosh from four loose sections at once, something there is no sense doing again."

The Movers

We have come back to a house
In Centralia, its body
Boarded and locked, and we have
Come for the last time, loading
The things we have lived without.
They are heavy with weather,
Slush and smoke, the back yard vent
Shaping our share of the fire
Into a column. We are
Not speaking though we are words
Leaving the oil that burns
Inside rain, but we have come
Back to fill ourselves part-way
And be satisfied though we
Will dry before dark, tables
And beds behind us in trucks.
As flammable as our land,
As breathless as our basement,
We gut this house slowly and
Retreat to the road, driving
The detour until the first
Fissure yawns in our red past.

Claude Wertz

"This is a town where every liquor store box is hauled off to be packed with clothes, dishes, books. My father has taken up shouting; my mother has taken to church. Which makes me sneer, both of them, because Art Rooker talks of rifles each time a commission examines us. He says, 'We should empty each body of words,' and yesterday I learned the paragraphs of Shirley Weaver's life when her story ran in the paper after her monoxide alarm malfunctioned: I learned her neighbors joked about 'Shirley's Schoolhouse' because of the frequent bells; I learned anger was nothing like one of those fist-fights with some local jerk. The manufacturer's explanation ran down the column beside Shirley's picture until it turned to blood."

The Tourists

Now Route 61 has cracked
And these dry geyser
Steam clouds do not subtract
Vision in a dream of faults.
Now the soap smooth voice
At the press conference
Washes itself and leaves
Before the village sinks,
An unlucky oiled bird.

So we take a camera walk
And feel like poachers, think
Of the deer with the arrow
In its head that made
The paper last week, how,
Surrounded by fence, it shared
The West Aliquippa curse,
Backed up to Ohio by trains. **

Look, we laughed about that island,
The necessary overpass, and half
The roads here are closed.
A winter of no snow
Squats over Pennsylvania

And refuses to go,
And we take pictures
And listen to the grocer say,
"Twenty-three years we've been
Sleeping with a leper.
Twenty-three years we've been
Waking up surprised
Our faces are falling off."
We nod and expect a toll gate,
Someone ringing a contagious bell.

Art Rooker

"He was drunk at his wife's funeral. He spoke aloud when he meant to whisper, and that night, glass in hand, he made me walk with him into this vented field. There was a kind of half-light we had grown used to, knowing that a mile away the clear sky would not surprise us, draped at one end as if that window were ragged and broken. This time, standing beside him as he scuffed the soil for footing, I thought the moon was searching for us, a weak-battery flashlight that could never make anything out for certain, and whoever was holding it would have to call out and give himself away, saying something stupid like 'Is that you?' or 'Who's there?' It could have been a couple of minutes that he took to get his feet in place, shifting in tiny increments like wrist wrestlers trying to get that slim advantage of leverage. The nearest pipe was ten yards away. Another one stood twenty yards off. It was like walking on a factory roof except you had to imagine the looking down to where men would be busy when the shift-change came. 'Right now,' he said, 'we're the opposite of Noah, standing here on the first piece of the earth to die.' I wished I had brought a bottle with me—I had nothing to do with my hands except stick them in my pockets."

The Stayers

We have begun to think like snakes,
Aware of how we touch the earth,
And the copperheads have taught us,
Dragging our fear through Centralia.

Uneven, this crust over fire.
We watch our shoes for the sinking
First sign of collapse, and the snakes
Inside us swim on the soil.

The copperheads speak of surface.
These refugees talk through winter,
Disregard their blood. Subsidence.
Monoxide. Venom. Everything

Is feeding our choice. We coil.
We watch the smoke-fissure highway
Conceal each cracked house's travel.
Below us the copperheads are
Thinking of coal, thinking of feet.

Donny Knouse

"Later, I told her, as we lay on the unnatural warm earth, that we were becoming a national anecdote, and her expression explained that she did not understand me. So I let it pass, imagining I could hear the fire underneath the soil, watching for something to change on her face which was almost lit by the light that flared beneath us."

> ** West Aliquippa, Pennsylvania, is said to be the only inland town in the United   States that can be entered or left in just one direction.

Bourbon, Red Meat, Salt, Grease

"I've been running mornings," my friend says,
"Trying to break even with the bourbon
And the red meat." I swat whatever is biting
At twilight and hold the last beer I'm having
Because I stop at eight. "All that salt,"
He says. "All that grease. I give myself
An hour on the highway to sweat it out."

His neighbor is watching us. He's maybe seventy,
And he's not holding a drink or playing
A doo-wop tape. I check him for a hair shirt;
I don't believe my friend is saving one day
Of his life by running, but I say, "Listen
To those guys singing their hearts out,"
Meaning Jackie and the Starlites, who are
Only begging for Valerie to come back,
Not a reprieve from chest pain, another morning
To wake up thinking, "That's the last time."

Ants

In 1952, at a family picnic, my aunt
Warned me not to sleep on the grass.
She said ants would crawl up my nose
And told the story of a woman she knew
With an anthill in her forehead, how
She'd slept outside and, unknowing,
Woken with ants in her sinuses.

I was ready to start second grade,
Old enough, you'd think, to disbelieve
Something, but I brushed myself
While I listened to the rest
Of that victim's problems: her operation
To clear a colony of ants that had settled
On a kind of satellite, accepting
Those tunnels as home. I stared down
And saw how the grass teemed, how there
Were nightmares of ants that would explore
My head and approve. My uncles sat down
To cards; my aunt started to make that grove
Look like we'd never been there, and
I kept walking and brushing myself
Like someone half-trained at putting out
Fire, refusing to drop and roll, but
Not running like a cindered fool.

Skid Marks

The driver shouted, "You big, dumb, shitty bastard!"
And the rush-hour lane jammed up behind his braked Ford.
I kept running, wouldn't turn to confirm how right
He was to curse at some stupid thirteen year-old
Who couldn't carry a newspaper home unhurt.
Horns ripped back the line while I made the corner
And escaped the unlit tunnel of Butler Street
Where truckloads of winter ash fogged upward from tires.
In April, I knew, the patronage street sweepers
Took care of that kind of filth, but the driver's words
Did no more good than my father's. They never help;
They change us less than news reports or one of those
Force-fed prom-night slaughter films screened in driver's ed.
So this week it's my son at the end of skid marks
That swerved wild-left enough to leave him sprawled but whole.
Nobody screamed at him, but half an hour later
I saw the skid ended at the edge of something
I couldn't trace, and I backed off from that dark ice,
Thought things had turned hollow under that thin pavement
While I'd step-guessed the speed that had tumbled my son
Before it could wear away like language, "You big,
Dumb, shitty bastard!" spit into the world again,
However much I'd warned him. I calculated
Forty miles per hour and walked home to fail, among
The van-line boxes, to break my record for darts,
Flinging the last red one sidearm into the waste
Of another sold house, and Christ, I missed the bull's
Huge body of my stacked trash, launching that dart through
An off-season storm door, starting chain reactions
Along a million tiny etchings that opened
Inward to the floor. It could have been the teacher's
Space shuttle. I'd wanted, a year before, to choose
Myself from all those applicants, sabbatical
For space; I'd taught one semester of weightless dreams,
Tuned them into a fool's stack of diamonds, shattered
Storm-window; I'd run replays of the Challenger
And pointed to every flaw and mistake, shouting,

"You big, dumb, shitty bastard!" at every NASA
Spokesman; and this afternoon I carried boxes,
Relocating again, setting up inside walls
I believe built for my arthritis, my asthma,
My habit of redressing the streets, dashing back
For thirty year-old papers, the Eisenhower
Promises, two more years of benign neglect.
This time I turn and retrace myself to the Ford's
Blue door; this time I yank it open and startle
My fist through the driver's words, as if shutting him
Up would accomplish some partial good, as if each
Unseen auto would skid and veer before it churned
Over whichever one of us is caught dreaming
On the highway, gawking up or behind ourselves,
Big, dumb, shitty bastards, epithets of travel.

The Red Health

After bean soup, after split buttered rolls
And the first helping of meat and gravy,
After potatoes and gravy, filling and gravy,
After waffles and gravy and a second helping
Of everything wiped up with bread so only
The thin grease film sparkles on the plate,
After that Sunday dinner, two kinds of pie
Baked by thick-armed women who bring the flush
Up in their men's faces because the red health
Has eaten here for years, because the red health
Fills out fists and breasts by thirteen and from
That feeding, the first fierce summer darkness
In the farm's lie-down-together groves,
The waking to eggs and bacon, pancakes and sausage
And the sweet sopping up with hand-sliced bread,
The turning out for work, the inheritance of earth,
The truth of growth, and from all of these families,
From all of these cousins choosing each other
And reinforcing the local names into a hopeless
Phone book repetition, the red health covers,
County by county, these Pennsylvania farms,
Lifts the hand to the chest, slaps the mouth open,
Folds the legs under the sudden candor of weight
While from one kitchen to the next to the tables
Where the red health gathers, they celebrate
What they've made from the industry of abundance.

From **THE DAYS OF UNCERTAIN HEALTH**
(1988)

The Girl who Breathes through a Hole in her Neck

The girl who breathes through a hole in her neck
Fills the library with mortality.
She makes us turn, keeps us from our reading;
She is the only one who concentrates.
Her deep breaths make us listen to our hearts,
Our breathing shallow as she approaches
Like the stalking skeleton with the scythe
We see in holiday weekend papers.
We are not on the bleak highway yet feel
Control slipping away. If there were a pole
Or an oncoming car we would hit it.
She reads, perhaps no longer hears herself.
It is a blessing we are not sharing.
The readers in this room are fast thinning.
This town will soon grow ignorant and she
Will be left well-read, a dread genius
In our midst reciting as she passes.

Quagmire

Outside of town, the soft bog
Digests those things that die there.
We test it with our shoes, imagine
Hands upraised and the lungs filled,
The body deep brown like the emblem
Of a sinking, strangled country.

Our nervous dog knew someone, perhaps,
Who foundered here like those mammoths
And sharp-fanged tigers on every
Museum wall. In this quagmire, smother
Is a sign of spring; summer tempts us
To dig for our original selves, the bones
And weapons lost under our cautious feet.

Soon something may surface. The swamp,
A local farmer tells us, is spreading,
Bleeding out from this black wound.
Our house is downhill from here;
The Earth may be tipping. Some night
After a March thaw we will hear
The gurgling of a million lost voices
Thick with slime. Slipping under the door,
They will bubble and multiply, rising,
Like ancestry, toward a common ceiling.

Interior

Across the room a woman asked for tea.
She was crying. We noticed this like stains
On the silver, a child whining for cake.

And though she gestured to the stoic man,
We waited for her voice to rise, longing
For delicious complaint. The moment passed.
She did not begin as we predicted;
Nothing could have changed her bored companion.
Already he looked at his watch, the tea,
At last, arrived, and the blue room was filled
With our fantasies of his new lover.

Coming in from the street, two girls approached;
One of them carried flowers. The knotted
Scene was funeral, wedding, birth, or tryst.
The thin candles on their table flickered
On like apprehension, like appetite.

Street Cleaning

I have been thinking of the woman
Who died before we moved here, her cough
Coloring with pain through the Fall:

That first night we slept on the floor,
Our furniture in New Jersey.
My throat went out again, my voice
Unnoticed along the curb where cars
Were positioned like confirmation
Of rumors. Before dawn the haunting
Of our street began: the husband
In the house is dismantling hope;
The children have colds; a neighboring
Village is chronically burning.

It is the woman who died before we moved here.
It is the woman who watched the sun turn wound-red,
Tear, like flesh, near the horizon. And we are
Waiting across the street, unsure of dawn,
Paper birds circling our son's crib.

We eat her pickles, the woman who died before we moved here.
The children tease the sleeping ants with crumbs. About ten o'clock,
The factory unsubtle, black smoke pours over the town.
There is no remedy. Sloshing through
The pre-Christmas snow, we notice
The fine-ground pepper fallout, the off-white
Of something not quite certain: a fault, a crack
In the lungs opening like a miserable seam in our clothing.

In this town the streets are regularly cleaned,
The science-fiction sucking sound outside
Our window at three, at four; things disposed of,
Gone into autopsy like unexpected deaths.

Month of Sundays

The minister of brimstone
Is taking my children
To hell, is describing
My place in the flame-flushed
Night of regret, and I
Tell them I have changed,
Insist I am alive, cold,
And the light outside
Is not the devil's ruse.
I am explaining like
A child backed by bullies
Against the schoolyard fence,
The teacher inside smoking,
And I tell them the fire
Is an infant's dream, our
Hot feet a baby's game,
And I am denying the smoke
From my pockets, the fine ash
We are forced to inhale.
We are snow, we are winter,
We are these white bodies
That have deep inside them
The sinless heart fire, yes.

Winner of the 2003 Flannery O'Connor Award for Short Fiction, the 2003 Ohio State University/The Journal Poetry Prize, the 2010 Stephen F. Austin Poetry Prize, and the 2015 Jacar Press Poetry Prize for book manuscripts, Gary Fincke has published twenty-nine books of short fiction, poetry, and nonfiction as well as the 2014 novel How Blasphemy Sounds to God. Individual poems and stories have won the Bess Hokin Prize from Poetry, the Rose Lefcowitz Prize from Poet Lore, the George Garrett Prize from Willow Springs, and two Pushcart Prizes. He is the Charles Degenstein Professor of English and Creative Writing at Susquehanna University.

Bringing Back the Bones: New and Selected Poems

Acknowledgments

From *A Week of Uncertain Health:* **Lynx House Press**
The Girl who Breathes through   *Poetry*
a Hole in her Neck
Quagmire   *Yarrow*
Interior   *Serendipity Arts*
Street Cleaning   *Memphis State Review*
Month of Sundays   *The GW Review*

From *Plant Voices:*   **Yardbird Books**
Sleeping with the Leper   *Beloit Poetry Journal*
What the Builder Left   *The Gettysburg Review*
Skid Marks   *Mid-American Review Groaning*
Boards   *The Georgia Review*
The Red Health   *Long Pond Review*
Bourbon, Red Meat, Salt Grease   *Poetry*
Ants   *Prairie Schooner*

From *The Double Negatives of the Living:* **Zoland Books**
Naming the Sky   *Poetry Northwest*
The Congestive Failure of Belief *Poetry Northwest*
The Double Negatives of the Living *Poetry*
Reaching the Deaf   *Poetry*
The Stuttering Cures   *Poetry*
The Flower Remedies   *Poetry Northwest*
Six Kinds of Music, the Wallpaper of Breasts *Beloit Poetry Journal*

From *Inventing Angels:*   **Zoland Books**
A Murder of Crows   *Poetry*
The Book of Numbers   *Poetry Northwest*
The Wonder Children   *Poetry Northwest*
The Butterfly Effect   *Green Mountains Review*
Oxygen   *The Literary Review*
The Theories for Ball Lightning   *Pennsylvania Rev./Zone 3*
The Skill of the Sunlight's Good *The Gettysburg Review*
The Congestive Failure of Belief *Poetry Northwest*
Every Reachable Feather   *Poetry Northwest*

The Early History of the Submarine — *The Paris Review*
Otherwise Healthy — *Mid-American Review*
The Plagues in Order — *Smartish Pace*
Birds-of-Paradise — *North American Review*
How's It Going? — *Two Rivers Review*
The Magpie Evening: A Prayer — *Prairie Schooner*

From ***Standing around the Heart:*** **Univ. of Arkansas Press**
Standing around the Heart — *The Paris Review*
The Eternal Language of the Hands — *The Paris Review*
The Buchinger Limbs — *The Southern Review*
The Uses of Rain — *The Missouri Review*
The History of Silk — *Western Humanities Rev.*
Anniversary — *The Southern Review*
The Weaknesses of the Mouth — *The Southern Review*
Sweet Things — *DoubleTake*
Headcheese, Liverwurst, a List of Loaves — *The Gettysburg Review*
Coughing through the Brambles — *The Missouri Review*
Miss Hartung Teaches Us the Importance of Fruit — *The Paris Review*
Johnny Weismuller Learns the Tarzan Yell — *The Paris Review*
The History of SAC — *Boulevard*
In Films, the Army Ants are Always Intelligent — *Poetry Northwest*

From ***The Fire Landscape:*** **Univ. of Arkansas Press**
The Anomaly Museum — *The Gettysburg Review*
Black Veils — *Prairie Schooner*
The Pause in the Plummet for Prayer — *Gettysburg Review*
The Sorrows — *Southern Poetry Review*
The Horns of Guy Lombardo — *Prairie Schooner*
False Dawn — *Michigan Quarterly Review*
White Gloves — *Prairie Schooner*
Like Ours — *Prairie Schooner*
The 1918 House — *The Gettysburg Review*

From ***Reviving the Dead:*** **Time Being Books**
Telling the Bees — *The Southern Review*
Evaluation — *Chariton Review*
For Good — *Hampden-Sydney Poetry*
Scattering — *Prairie Schooner*
Translating the Hawk — *Prairie Schooner*

From *The History of Permanence:*

The Serious Surprise of Sorrow	*Alaska Quarterly Review*
The Etymology of Angels	*The Missouri Review*
After the Aberfan Disaster	*Gettysburg Review*
Things that Fall from the Sky	*Beloit Poetry Journal*
The Possibilities for Wings	*Virginia Quarterly Review*
Selfless	*Virginia Quarterly Review*
Specificity	*Gettysburg Review*
The Dead Girls	*Ploughshares*
Meat Eaters	*Alaska Quarterly Review*

Stephen F. Austin University Press

The Light: New Poems

Prelude	*River Styx*
The Danger of Yawing	*Alaska Quarterly Review*
Fraternity Brothers: 1970	*Beloit Poetry Journal*
Light	*Southern Quarterly*
The Drive-Thru Strip Club	*River Styx*
The Mathematics of Ecstasy	*Tampa Review*

Inventing Angels was reprinted in *Harper's*

Parts 1 and 3 of The Great Chain of Being were reprinted in *Harper's*

The Era of the Vari-Vue appeared in *The Pushcart Prize, Volume XX*

Light Enough to be Lifted was reprinted in the *Anthology of Magazine Verse, 1997*

The Natural Method of Dog Training was reprinted in *The Best of 20 Years of Verse*

The History of Silk was reprinted by the *Academy of American Poets*

Class A, Salem, The Rookie League was reprinted in *Motion: American Sports Poems*

What the Builders Left was reprinted in *The State Street Reader*

Oxygen was cited by *The Pushcart Prize*

The Buchinger Limbs was reprinted on *Verse Daily*

The Sorrows was reprinted on *Poetry Daily* and read on NPR by Garrison Keillor

Standing around the Heart, The Eternal Language of the Hands, The Uses of Rain, Sweet Things, and In Films, the Army Ants are Always Intelligent were reprinted in *Poetry Magazine.com*

The Dark Angels was reprinted in *Intersections*

CPSIA information can be obtained
at www.ICGtesting.com
Printed in the USA
FSOW01n1134111216
28435FS